RAILS
IN THE
HINTERLAND

New Zealand's Vanishing Railway Landscape

Dedication

This book is dedicated to the memory of three good friends:
Alan Bellamy (1923-2004),
George Emerson (1935-2002)
and my brother Ross McQueen (1927-2004).
All were notable railway or tramway historians, recorders and photographers, and exceptionally generous in helping others of like interests.

RAILS IN THE HINTERLAND

New Zealand's Vanishing
Railway Landscape

Euan McQueen

GRANTHAM HOUSE
NEW ZEALAND

Unless otherwise noted, all photographs were taken by the author.

First published 2005

GRANTHAM HOUSE PUBLISHING
6/9 Wilkinson Street
Oriental Bay
Wellington
New Zealand

ISBN 1 86934 094 9

Edited by Lorraine Olphert

Designed by Graham Stewart, Bookprint Consultants Limited, Wellington.

Printed by Bookprint International Limited, Hong Kong.

Contents

Acknowledgments

Most of the photographs in this book are my own. But there were a few critical gaps, ably filled by contributions from the late Alan Bellamy's collection (via his son Darryl), Dave Turner, the late George Emerson (via Ingrid and Richard Emerson) and, via my publisher Graham Stewart, Derek Cross photographs from the W.W. Stewart collection. Aidan Challis thoughtfully offered the rare photograph taken from a car on the Waitaki road-rail bridge.

Kerry Sellers was helpful with typing parts of the text. Anne White and her team at Elite Secretarial Ltd performed the required rites with their customary efficiency to bring the manuscript together in an ordered and intelligible form. Graham Stewart of Grantham House was always available to advise, exhort and otherwise counsel his part-time author. John Whibley gave material assistance with updating maps; Trevor Terry, of Hamilton, was always ready with prompt answers to my questions; Alan Smith and Bill Cowan provided information in areas of their special interests; my late brother Ross was instructive on bush trams and logging techniques; George Teesdale, of Runanga, told me about coal distribution in the area. Mike Mellor provided valuable comment at the final stages of writing the book, with an eagle eye for fact, expression and punctuation. And there are others who knowingly and unknowingly supported, advised and encouraged as the book developed.

My wife, Noeline, forever patient and tolerant, lived for many months with paper and photographs in unusual places in our small home. To her I owe a special debt of gratitude and affection.

I am grateful to you all.

Foreword

For the last 45 years I have photographed the New Zealand landscape both urban and rural – and in particular the railway landscape, with its furniture and fittings. For much of the period the railway was an integral part of that broader landscape. Trains and locomotives were photographed only if they happened to be there; they are certainly interesting, but only as part of the bigger picture. I wanted to capture the whole railway, not just the mobile bit, and in particular the ordinary scenes that defined the New Zealand railway landscape.

Over more recent years I have given many illustrated talks about the railway landscape, with my interpretation of why it was there and why it was changing (and disappearing), especially in the last three decades of the 20th century. The talks were given to railway groups and, more particularly, to audiences with more general interests.

It was the latter groups in particular who encouraged me to write about the themes developed during the talks: of a railway as part of the local community; of the distinctive architecture and style of railway buildings and structures; of how the railway worked; and, to some degree, what it meant to work on 'the railway'. I am grateful for that prompting, and as a result this book is addressed as much to the lay audience as it is to those already steeped in railways and trains.

It is a personal selection of photographs, mainly my own, but complemented by a few from others' collections, including some who have also come to develop the view that a railway is much more than trains and locomotives. If the photographs are not always crystal clear, it is the result of the passage of time and the variable quality of some film.

This is not just a book of photographs. It is a book about a vital part of the national transport network in its second century of operation, how it served local communities and needs, and what it looked like in its day-to-day life in performing that service. The commentary with each photograph is designed to explain what is in the photograph and how it fits in to the broader context of the system, without getting too technical about operational matters.

It is, of course, but one person's selection, governed by choice and availability of photographs. It lays no claim to a complete geographic coverage. There are others with comparable or better collections – their work appears in journals, calendars and books. Perhaps, over time, some of them will be encouraged to put together and publish their photographic choices of railway landscapes over the years, covering other regions and eras.

The railway and its role is a topic inclined to be taken for granted in New Zealand's social and economic history. There is still much to reach the public eye. I hope this book goes some way towards filling that gap.

Euan McQueen

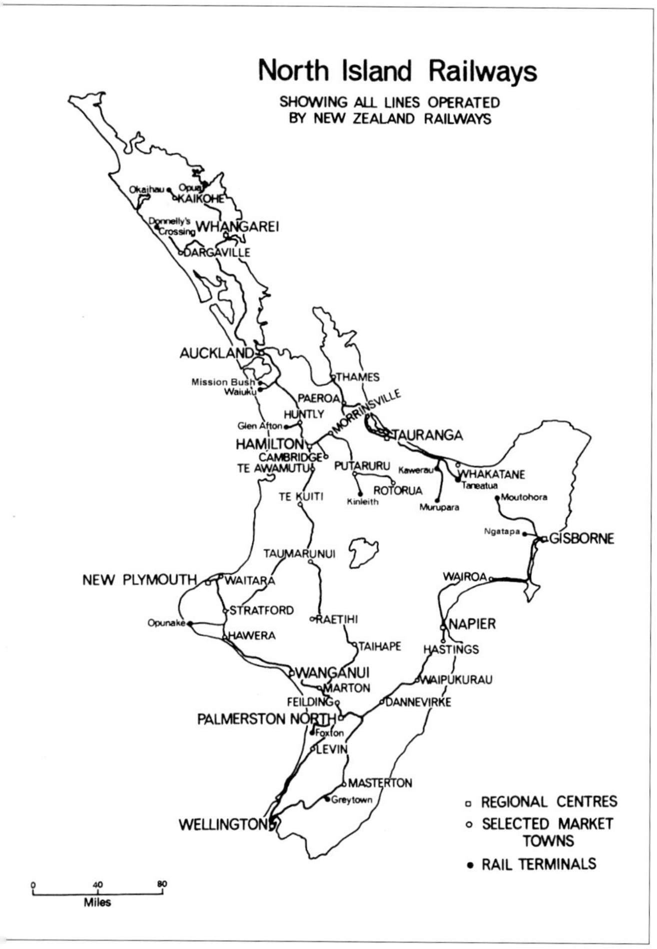
North Island Railways
SHOWING ALL LINES OPERATED BY NEW ZEALAND RAILWAYS
Okaihau
Opua
KAIKOHE
Donnelly's Crossing
WHANGAREI
DARGAVILLE
AUCKLAND
Mission Bush
Waiuku
THAMES
PAEROA
MORRINSVILLE
HUNTLY
Glen Afton
HAMILTON
TAURANGA
CAMBRIDGE
TE AWAMUTU
PUTARURU
Kawerau
WHAKATANE
Taneatua
ROTORUA
TE KUITI
Kinleith
Murupara
Moutohora
Ngatapa
GISBORNE
TAUMARUNUI
NEW PLYMOUTH
WAITARA
WAIROA
STRATFORD
Opunake
RAETIHI
NAPIER
HAWERA
TAIHAPE
HASTINGS
WANGANUI
WAIPUKURAU
MARTON
FEILDING
DANNEVIRKE
PALMERSTON NORTH
Foxton
LEVIN
MASTERTON
Greytown
WELLINGTON
REGIONAL CENTRES
SELECTED MARKET TOWNS
RAIL TERMINALS
0
40
80
Miles

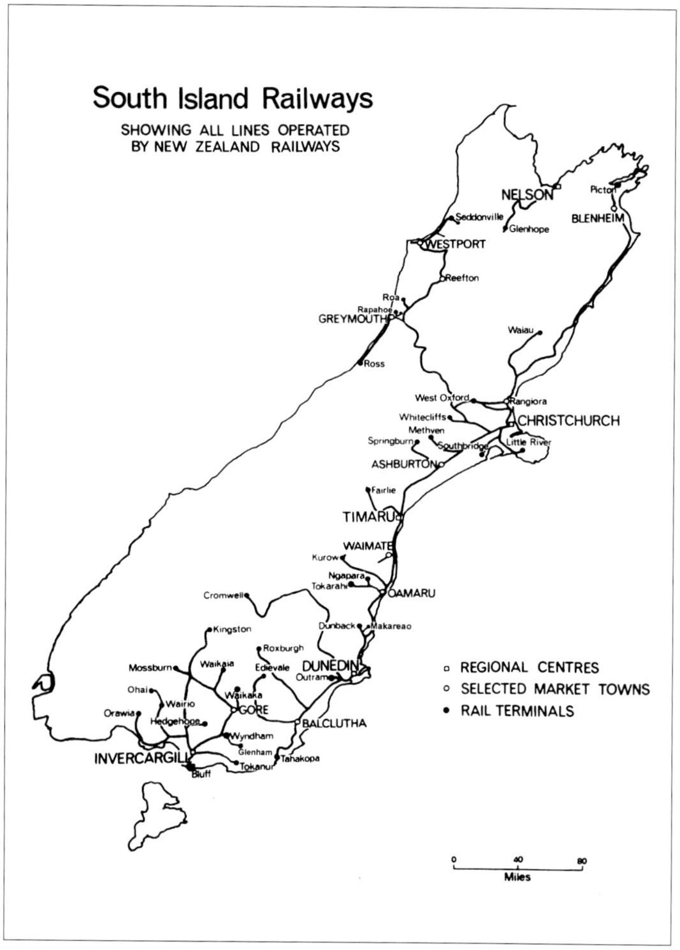
South Island Railways
SHOWING ALL LINES OPERATED BY NEW ZEALAND RAILWAYS
NELSON
Picton
Seddonville
Glenhope
BLENHEIM
WESTPORT
Reefton
Roa
Rapahoe
GREYMOUTH
Waiau
Ross
West Oxford
Rangiora
Whitecliffs
CHRISTCHURCH
Methven
Springburn
Southbridge
Little River
ASHBURTON
Fairlie
TIMARU
WAIMATE
Kurow
Ngapara
Tokarahi
OAMARU
Cromwell
Dunback
Makareao
Kingston
Roxburgh
Mossburn
Waikaia
Edievale
DUNEDIN
Outram
Ohai
Waikaka
Wairio
Orawia
Hedgehope
GORE
BALCLUTHA
Wyndham
Glenham
INVERCARGILL
Tokanui
Tahakopa
Bluff
REGIONAL CENTRES
SELECTED MARKET TOWNS
RAIL TERMINALS
0
40
80
Miles

Introduction

For several decades until the 1960s, New Zealand's national railway network was in a relatively steady state. A few branch lines had closed in the early 1930s, a few more in the 1950s, and railways to Kinleith (1950) and Murupara (1957) were opened. In 1953 the maximum route length was reached – 5689 kilometres – but then began a steady and inexorable decline over subsequent decades as branch lines closed. From 1945 to 1955 total route length reduced by only 11 kilometres; from 1955 to 1965 the net reduction was 378 kilometres. The trend was to continue, until in 2004 there were 4103 route kilometres of railway on the national network, a reduction of 1586 kilometres since 1953.

The scope and nature of the railway system's operation in the initial period also saw little change. Remaining passenger services were being withdrawn from some branch lines, a few stations were closed, but most effort was assigned to moving growing freight tonnage in the post-World War II years as increased prosperity created new transport demands. It was a period of major land development projects. Increasing quantities of fertiliser and lime were required for these projects, and transport needed for the eventual livestock and wool. The growth in demand for industrial and consumer goods kept steady pressure on a network that was still struggling to get over the heavy demands of the war years. Labour and materials had been scarce in that period; significant recovery of asset quality on the railway was not to come until the 1970s.

The railway system in the 1950s was still oriented to meeting local and rural needs as much as toward longer inter-regional haulage. Since 1936 competition from road transport for freight alongside an open railway had been limited by law to 30 miles (48 kilometres) for all but a few commodities, or for freight moved with a special permit.

With this degree of protection from road competition the Railways Department was thus obliged to serve the many small communities and farming areas along its network. In 1952 there were some 1060 stations handling general freight on the network, plus many private sidings serving a single user. The South Island had 560 of these stations, the North Island 500. There were, in addition, over 150 small stations without freight sidings, handling passengers, parcels and small lots – consignments that could be handled by one man from the train to the station shelter shed. In many areas these small flag stations were well used into the 1960s for parcels and smaller consignments: mail, groceries, newspapers, boxes of fruit and sacks of seed were all frequently seen, especially on routes where roads were poor.

Today (2004), there are 18 freight centres where all types of freight are handled, plus a few score private sidings for individual users and another small group of stations which see use for bulk freight traffic such as logs. The only small stations remaining without freight sidings are those used by commuters in the Wellington and Auckland regions, and a few on long-distance passenger routes.

In 1952 there were 74 stations between Christchurch and Dunedin with sidings handling general freight, plus numerous private sidings. In 2004 there are four such stations (Ashburton, Temuka, Timaru and Oamaru) plus a few major private sidings serving particular industries away from these stations. A few other stations, such as Washdyke, Studholme and Palmerston, still have sidings and will handle bulk consignments in multiple wagon-loads as required. And the nine rural branch lines that left the Main South Line between Christchurch and Dunedin in 1953 had all closed by 2002, taking with them some 75 stations. Trucks, both those linked to the railway operation and those operating independently, now provide the freight transport needs for those areas.

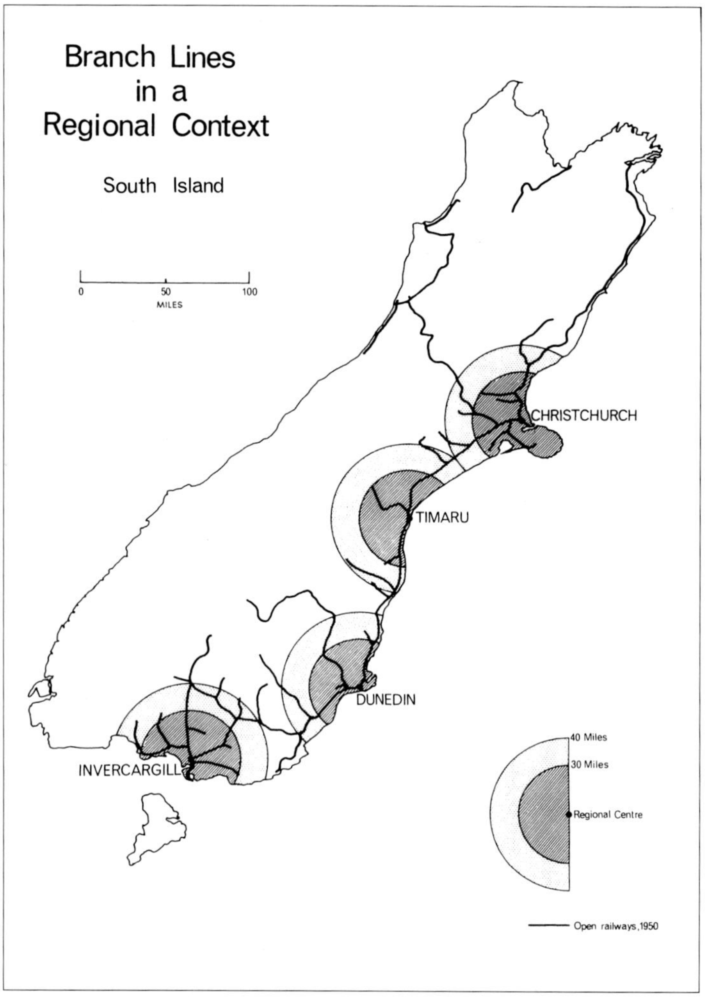

The Reasons for Change

The factors that brought about such change in the second half of the 20th century are many and varied. Key elements included:

Major advances in the capabilities of commercial road freight, with bigger and more efficient equipment becoming available. This trend applied particularly from the 1970s onward.

The progressive reduction of competitive restrictions between road and rail in stages from 1961 to their complete abolition in the mid-1980s.

The map on the facing page illustrates in a general way the proximity of many branch line stations, and rural stations on the main railway routes, to regional centres such as Christchurch, Timaru, Dunedin and Invercargill. The arcs around each centre portray the approximate distances within which each railway was protected from most road competition (30 miles/48 kilometres) to May 1963, when it was extended to 40 miles (64 kilometres) and from 1977 to 150 kilometres. The map shows clearly that the zones of influence of the regional centres left few branch lines beyond the 64-kilometre limit.

These generally longer routes were among the later closures: Waiau in 1978, Otago Central (beyond Middlemarch) in 1990, Tapanui in 1978 (and then prompted by flood damage); Kingston, which carried only light freight traffic, lasted until 1982 as the route of the Kingston Flyer tourist train.

The North Island had far fewer branch lines and a different distribution of regional centres. The main routes run through the main farming regions, rather than along the coastal boundaries as in Otago and Canterbury. But the impact on rural stations on the main lines was the same, and for the same reasons.

There were significant changes in freight-handling practices on farms and in factories, timber mills and other industries. For example, from the mid-1960s on, most grain was handled in bulk, rather than in bags. Farm storage incentives became available to reduce the intensive peak of activity at the annual harvest, which then relied largely on the railway and local stations to get grain to flour mills as it was harvested. Potatoes were increasingly handled in bins, rather than sacks. Forklifts and pallets became the norm for most freight handling. These and other efficiencies led to the centralisation of handling, production and processing in many industries, such as seed processing, flour milling, timber production and coal handling. The demand on local railway facilities to meet the needs of farmers and smaller towns diminished; and often railway wagons and older rail-served factories did not match the needs of the new handling techniques.

Some traffic virtually disappeared. Coal carried by rail to dairy factories and other plants in the North Island was replaced largely by natural gas supplied via pipelines in the 1960s and 70s. Coal gas plants all over New Zealand disappeared from the 1960s to the 1980s, and with it the significant tonnage of coal carried by rail. Coal-fired steam locomotives disappeared from the network in 1971 after a progressive change to diesel power over the previous two decades. Domestic coal demand diminished sharply as the use of coal ranges reduced and open fires were replaced by more efficient wood burners fed by local firewood, rather than coal from a distant mine.

The rationalisation of the dairy industry saw, from the 1960s, a progressive reduction in the number of dairy factories. Where once there were seven factories along the Opunake branch in Taranaki, by the 1970s there was only one specialist plant at Kapuni. Dairy processing in the southern half of the North Island was increasingly concentrated at three plants at Whareroa (south of Hawera), Longburn (near Palmerston North) and Pahiatua. Whareroa today draws milk from all over this area (much of it by rail). This is traffic on an industrial scale; it is no longer local, where the farmer can see his production go out from the local station and the coal come in to 'his' dairy factory via the same station.

Ports, from the 1970s on, experienced major change in their demands on railways. The 'railway port', including most of the South Island ports, had began to change cargo-handling practices by the mid-1960s so that there was very little of the short haul and costly traffic between ship's side and local store or goods sheds. It was not unusual in 1959 to have up to 1400 wagons stored under load around Christchurch after a 12-kilometre haul from ships unloaded at Lyttelton. It was inefficient, costly and not what a modern railway was really about. Change had to happen – and it did from the early 1960s on. From the 1970s local traffic to and from ports was increasingly in containers handled in a terminal behind the port, or by truck. Wagons at ship's side are now a rare sight – and the many small private sidings and small stations in both urban and rural areas to handle this short haul traffic became redundant.

In rural areas (not only on branch lines) there was a further significant change: the release of any restrictions on livestock cartage in 1961, which saw the railway's role in that traffic disappear in the 1970s apart from a few trial loadings in 1994.

The progressive disappearance of traditional coastal shipping in the years following the introduction of the rail ferries in 1962 saw much of the local farm output, particularly within Canterbury and North Otago, transfer from rail to road. Traditionally, potatoes and other produce would have been in sacks, loaded into wagons at stations such as Willowbridge or Waimate or St Andrews and railed to the 'railway' port at Oamaru or Timaru. Some of this freight continued to go by rail but direct from a central place, such as Methven (in the 1970s), Ashburton or Christchurch to the North Island via the rail ferries. And it was increasingly in bins or in bulk. If it was in sacks it was handled by forklift, rather than muscle. This in turn called for a new wagon fleet, with the ability to handle pallets and the associated loading by forklift.

The free or cheap railage of lime, which produced many thousands of tonnes of traffic each year for Railways in the 1950s, much of it to smaller stations, was first reduced in scale then abolished in the early 1960s. There was no longer the incentive to keep a station close to the farm for this traffic.

All these changes were matched by a decline in rural towns' commercial activity and an associated population reduction, as the cities and regional centres grew bigger and took over smaller town functions. Improved roads and road transport were important elements in this change.

In summary, the need for local stations and local lines (branch lines) diminished and disappeared. It was not a decline in farm output but a change in handling and transport methods. It happened with fertiliser: as bulk depots at central points served large areas, the demand for bagged fertiliser in individual consignments diminished. The then Railways Department moved quickly to close smaller stations and, in time, to remove their track and buildings.

Some rural branch lines lasted longer, as major hydro-electric power schemes were built in their hinterlands. Roxburgh saw a period of intense activity as the dam beyond the branch terminus was built in the 1950s. (Some equipment for that project was delivered via the Waikaka branch.) The life of the Kurow branch was extended by its role in transporting material for the power scheme at Benmore in the Upper Waitaki. In the last decade of the Otago Central line's life beyond Middlemarch materials for the Clyde dam construction increasingly dominated the consists of trains until the line's closure in 1990. By that time most farm-based traffic was moving by road.

Thus, the local role of the railway progressively disappeared. The process began seriously in the 1960s and moved quickly through the 1970s and '80s. The closure of rural branch lines was but part of that process. In the 1990s larger centres like Levin, Feilding, Pukekohe, Taumarunui, Te Kuiti, Waipukurau, Balclutha, Gore and Westport lost their general freight role, leaving a few private sidings or bulk traffics handled by Tranz Rail. Stations within the main urban areas also lost their freight function, though not the passenger traffic in Auckland and Wellington regions. Papakura, Avondale, Lower Hutt, Upper Hutt, Rangiora, Burnside, all formerly busy stations, had their long-haul traffic brought into or taken from central urban freight centres by road. The use of container transfer between rail and road is relatively simple, and wagon utilisation improved sharply with fewer stations. But the offset was the loss of direct rail access for some industries, some of which simply switched to long-haul road transport, or coastal shipping plus trucks for inter-island traffic.

There have been many judgments and generalisations made about this trend. Few have rested on a knowledge of costs, prices and the hard information held only by customers, road transport operators or the railway operator.

Today, in 2004, it is a very different railway from the 1950s. There have been huge operational changes within that 50-year span – from steam to diesel, in signalling, in mechanised freight handling, in the scale and nature of passenger traffic, in the nature of competition and the perceived efficiencies of road transport, and in the qualities of management brought to all forms of transport. It is a tough, competitive, customer-driven industry – a far cry from the more informal, intimate and rather more relaxed style of 50 years ago.

The photographs and accompanying commentaries in this book attempt to portray some of the original railway operations and style in those more informal days. The word pictures I have painted to accompany the photographs are of a country where there was a railway station, however small, not too far away for all farmers near a railway route. And there were many more routes then than now. Even in 1959, *The Press* in Christchurch would note in farm sales advertisements "Handy to Rail", and the advertisements for many of Canterbury's ewe fairs included comments such as "Adequate rail wagons available" for the day of the sale.

These days are gone. If one yearns for their resurrection, it is but an exercise in nostalgia. They reflected a different pace of life, different transport technologies, an intimacy between rural areas and their railway, which was still the only truly national transport organisation and operator until probably the 1980s. It has been an inexorable change, not without a price to customers, communities, road users other than for freight, and those in the transport industry. But as with all progress, it had to happen. Today, the railway system carries more tonnes in a year than for any year before in its history. But these are different tonnes from earlier times, to and from different places and often in different and certainly much bigger wagons and trains.

This book is about scenes from the recent past, from the 1950s to a few vestigial remnants still extant even in the 21st century. For a comparison 'in the flesh' of the scale of these changes, one must visit railway heritage sites and compare the seemingly tiny wagons to the present fleet of 50-plus tonne capacity. Without changes such as those, there would now be only the remnants of the original railway system – or perhaps none at all.

Chapter One

RAILWAYS IN THE LANDSCAPE

New Zealand has a wide variety of land forms and landscapes. The railway builders have had to contend with a geologically young country, often prone to slips, slumps and deep or wide river crossings – and, as well, a climate subject to extremes of rain and wind.

The history of our railways is marked by low levels of funding for construction, a consequence of the small population. It is not surprising, therefore, that railway lines were built to follow the lie of the land, rather than taking an expensive alignment that minimised grades and curvature. There was not the financial resource to allow the level of expenditure needed to match the easy grades of railways in, for example, Britain, where a large population and high-density traffic supported the building of a quality alignment. This same principle – of a restricted fiscal base – is in 21st century New Zealand a constraint on building the arterial roads for which so many clamour.

The small selection of photographs that follows illustrates these points.

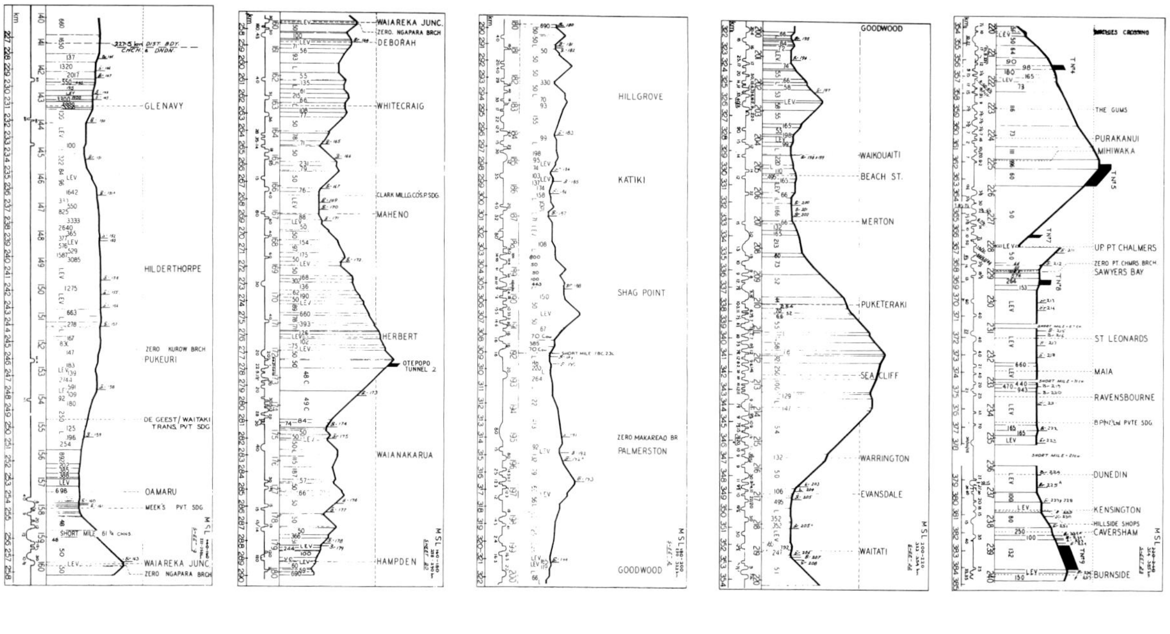

North Otago, 1960

The Main South Line, south of Oamaru, and especially near Dunedin, faces widely varying grades and curvature. The line follows the coastline at many points, taking advantage of the easier grades on the small coastal plain wherever possible. Even then there is a steep climb out of Oamaru and significant grades further south until the line reaches Sawyers Bay, 11 kilometres north of Dunedin. The grade diagrams on the facing page give an indication of both grades and curvature.

In the photograph the southbound Limited – the Monday-to-Saturday express running each way between Christchurch and Invercargill – is traversing the undulating country between Hillgrove and Katiki, some 30 kilometres north of Palmerston. The saltwater lagoon in the foreground lies between the promontory sheltering Moeraki from the southerlies (and on which the lighthouse stands).

It was a school holiday express, with about nine carriages (perhaps six second class, three first class), carrying families, children visiting relatives, business travellers and public servants. Behind the carriages would be a guards van full of luggage and then one or two large box wagons, one carrying mail, the other Post Office and Railways parcel traffic. The locomotive, designed by New Zealand Railways and built at Hillside workshop in the 1950s, worked the Timaru-Dunedin section. The Limited crossed its northbound counterpart at Katiki, a few kilometres south of this photograph, and here the locomotive and passenger crews changed over for the return to their respective bases at Invercargill and Christchurch (for passenger crew) and Dunedin and Timaru (for locomotive crew).

McDonald's Lime Company, Kakanui, 1960

When there were industrial activities away from the main line, the railway went to them – by a siding or a branch line. McDonald's Lime Company site – part of which appears in this photograph – was served by a private line, four kilometres long, which left the Whitecraig yard eight kilometres south of Oamaru and ran out across the rich North Otago soils to the lime-burning plant. The area was then, as it is still, renowned for its brassicas, as well as other vegetables.

Each working day a small steam locomotive would take lime, both raw and processed, down to Whitecraig station to be shunted on to main line trains, and return with empty wagons. Sometimes there would be a few wagons loaded with empty vegetable cases for the market gardeners; the wagons would be left at a gate on the 'main line' for unloading by the growers and then be picked up on the next trip to be taken back to the lime plant.

At the south end of Whitecraig yard the Totara Lime Company had a one-kilometre private line skirting a hill of limestone on the way to its quarry. Oamaru stone, in blocks, was extracted from there; there was also a lime crushing plant. This spur was worked by a horse; the line was evenly graded and did not pose problems for horse power.

These small extensions to the national system fitted into the local economy and landscape. The track occupied odd corners and the boundaries of a rich and productive area. The photograph shows wagons awaiting placement at the plant for loading, a derelict locomotive formerly used by McDonald's, some of the vehicles used on the site – and, of course, a large area of those famous brassicas along the North Otago coast just south of Oamaru. Both lines closed in 1965.

Waimate Branch, 1960

The Waimate branch opened in 1877 and closed in 1966. It was just over seven kilometres long and ran almost without a curve from the main line at Studholme Junction to Waimate. The only significant changes in alignment were a long curve coming out of Studholme and a short steep sharp curve coming into Waimate station. From 1885 to 1953 a branch line ran 13 kilometres from Waimate inland to Waihao Downs – the Waimate Gorge railway.

Branch lines in Canterbury were easy to build across the plains. With a good founding in gravels, formation maintenance was rarely a challenge. The rail in most cases was light (56 pounds to the yard, occasionally 70 pounds cascaded from the main line), and ballast would be drawn from local pits. They were relatively inexpensive to maintain, and the generally light traffic, in terms of train density and lower speeds, did not impose great demands.

This is the branch line, looking toward Waimate and showing the cattle stops at the State Highway One level crossing (behind the photographer), the back of the speed board warning of entry to Studholme, and the ubiquitous Railways pole line carrying the wires for New Zealand Railways' own national telephone and telegraph service (then second in size only to the Post Office network). The one-chain (20-metre) strip allocated to the railway corridor has the customary selection of weeds, occasionally burned off by the track gang or a spark from the branch train.

It is an entirely ordinary scene, replicated all over the country – though not often with such a long length of straight track. It is a micro landscape in its own right – for long an unobtrusive and routine part of New Zealand's rural landscape.

Esk Valley, Hawkes Bay, mid-1950s.

New Zealand is, in geological terms, a young country. This helps give rise to not only a varied topography but also in many areas land surfaces of considerable instability.

For railway builders, the often rugged hills of the North Island posed particular difficulties. Few routes presented such a challenge as the Napier-Gisborne railway. Although there were certainly easier stretches near Napier, south of Wairoa, and near Gisborne, the remainder passed through, over or around rugged and often very unstable country. The practice of landholders clear-felling bush sharply increased the risks of slips and subsidences, quite apart from adding to flood water flows and the silting of rivers.

From Eskdale to Waikoau (20 kilometres) was a steady climb, much of it at 1:60. There were three tunnels and innumerable curves, many of them sharp radius. More was to come 25 kilometres further on, with seven kilometres of steady 1:50 grade to Kotemaori.

This photograph, taken in the mid-1950s, shows the beginning of this long haul, as the railway runs out of the Esk Valley and begins the climb towards Waikoau. The sweeping curves are there to gain height; the train is a very small feature of the dominating landscape. *Derek Cross*

Maclennan, Catlins River Branch, South Otago, 1964

Although many branch lines were built into areas of native bush, in most cases the bush was quickly cleared and the main purpose of the line was to serve farmers.

The Catlins River line carried indigenous sawn timber for all its life, from 1885 to 1971. Certainly there were rich farmlands along the line from Balclutha to Owaka, reached in 1896, but from there on to the terminus at Tahakopa (69 kilometres from Balclutha) the grades were steep for much of the route, with a mix of native bush and hill country farms dominating the landscape.

The photograph is of Maclennan, the terminus of the line before it was opened to Tahakopa in 1915.

The major traffic from Maclennan and Tahakopa was, for many years, sawn indigenous timber from local sawmills. Maps show many bush trams in the area, some terminating at a nearby railway station where the sawmill was situated. Others brought timber to a mill in the bush, and the timber was taken to rail by bullock wagons or, later, trucks. Farming crept in over much of the felled areas but, as the photograph shows, many slopes reverted to scrub and second growth, especially on the south faces.

Maclennan in 1964 had the same look as the surrounding landscape – not much used and rather run down. A 1915 photograph shows a pristine station (with canopy), several houses nearby, an engine shed and smartly painted goods shed.

In 1964 the engine shed and houses (and sawmill) had well gone; the station had reduced in size and the large stockyards were overgrown. The road leading to the station was also becoming overgrown. There was still some traffic – fertiliser and small lots inward, timber and livestock outward, giving a total of close to 200 tonnes. Roads in the district, for long unreliable in winter, had become more robust and traditional railway traffic was switching to trucks. The track gang huts were still there; at this stage there were still four or five return trains a week, for which the gang provided safe track.

The distance of the Catlins River branch from major supply points and markets – mainly in and around Dunedin – helped hold much of the traffic to rail longer than for many other routes. But as the sawmills (mainly at Tahakopa) closed from the 1950s on, livestock was increasingly moved by road, and as the roads improved from a basic level, rail freight levels diminished steadily. Then development of a good road from Tahakopa to Wyndham in the 1960s diverted traffic from the bottom end of the line toward Wyndham and Invercargill.

It was a difficult line to build, in a rugged landscape for over half its length. The railway was critical to the area's settlement and development for perhaps 40-50 years, but then its utility diminished. Maclennan station, sitting under a classic Catlins landscape in 1964, is winding down.

Rochfort, 1967 – photograph on facing page at top.

Rochfort was on the 14-kilometre Raetihi branch, about three kilometres from the junction with the North Island Main Trunk at Ohakune. This short line, between two towns of similar size and function, spent much of its 51-year life carrying indigenous timber from Raetihi and the mill at Pakihi to urban centres. In later years it became an important livestock carrier, with store stock moving out of Raetihi for fattening on the lowlands. Other rural traffic, such as fertiliser and farm needs, supplemented this base load.

By the 1960s the timber traffic was light, and with competitive restrictions lifted and changing stock-buying practices, the stock traffic diminished. With Ohakune so close, and with more frequent train services on the main line, the branch steadily became of decreasing relevance.

Branch lines and other infrastructure in the community rarely become redundant suddenly. If it is clear that they have no long-term future, maintenance expenditure is minimised. When it is obvious that a local community no longer wants it, or significant money needs to be spent to keep it, the facility is closed.

This was the case with the Raetihi branch in 1967. Weed spraying, traditionally carried out twice a year, was no longer justified. Maintenance of the station building had ceased. Surprisingly, there was still some traffic using the sidings beneath the long grass on the left of the photograph. The Associated Bottlers Cooperative, which collected beer bottles at depots all over the North Island to send to Otahuhu for re-use at the nearby breweries, had its Ruapehu depot at Rochfort. Every few weeks a wagon was left there to load this traffic.

The remainder of the branch was in similar condition, and without too much fuss it was closed on 1 January 1968. Few remnants are left. Raetihi station, relocated from its original site, is the base for a local museum; a small timber truss bridge, still on the old formation, sits beside the state highway just south of Ohakune.

Ohakune is no longer a junction, even if the name has persisted over the years since 1968. The physical evidence of the Raetihi branch merged back into the rural landscape.

Gisborne, 1967

This is the railway in its urban landscape, on the coastal side of the city behind Waikanae Beach. It was still handling passenger traffic (the railcar is parked behind the station) and a lot of freight. The goods train in the yard is dominated by wagons used for carrying fertiliser, with covered wagons which would be used to carry processed vegetables from the nearby canning plant, and general freight. The green goods shed was one of the two inter-regional freight depots in town: this one for general freight to and from southern points, the other in the city operated by New Zealand Railways Road Services, which trucked freight north to the rail terminal at Taneatua for forwarding to northern destinations.

It was a busy regional terminal

then. The photograph does not show the large fertiliser depot at Matawhero (five kilometres to the west) or the fruit packing store at Makaraka (five kilometres away on the route of the old Moutohora branch), with its seasonal apple traffic. Nor does it show more than a few of the private sidings along the main line immediately west of the station serving warehouses, wool stores, bulk petrol installations, a road metal depot and other local firms that received their product from distant points or sent out local produce.

Behind the photographer, in 1967, were the port and the freezing works, a major source of outward traffic as an increasing proportion of its output was railed to ports at Napier and even Wellington. The Wattie's factory, just across the bridge in the foreground, was a significant user of rail services.

Since 2000 rail traffic on the Napier-Gisborne line has shrunk to low levels, although in 2004 there are encouraging signs of increased use. This reduction in traffic is not just due to diversion to road transport – some activities have simply disappeared or been transferred.

The freezing works closed; smaller works in the region, and the Wairoa plant, handle local livestock. Petrol was transferred to coastal tankers and now comes by road from Mt Maunganui or Napier. With a significant decline in sheep numbers, the wool clip has diminished. Consumer goods come from Auckland or other centres by truck direct to major outlets; there is a reduced need for the warehouses and the distribution role of the goods shed.

More road metal is trucked from points closer to Gisborne (for some years until 2001 chip for road sealing was railed from Wellington). Rail no longer services the freight needs of the port, where the major cargo is logs from Gisborne's immediate hinterland. And there has been some transfer of inward and outward freight from Napier/Hastings and points south to Tauranga/Auckland and points north. There is no feasible rail connection on the latter route.

The mainstays of the Gisborne rail traffic are now fertiliser from the manufacturing plant at Napier to the Matawhero depot, and outward container loads of local produce both for export and domestic use. There is also some sawn timber from local mills.

Passenger services to Gisborne ceased in the 1980s, but an excellent small steam-hauled tourist train operates from the former locomotive depot in the Gisborne yards. The heritage station hosts a weekend market and the tourist train, but little else. The impact of the railway on Gisborne's landscape is sharply diminished: many buildings in the yard have gone, the private sidings have disappeared (along with some of their owners), there are no staff based there in 2004. The many railway houses have all been sold. Perhaps, as governments look more seriously at road, rail and other infrastructure use, the route and stations will find a new long-term role. At present it is a tenuous existence, a rather sad but perhaps inevitable change in the local urban landscape.

Chapter Two

THE FARMERS' RAILWAY

The most widespread and long-term users of railways in the hinterland have been New Zealand's farmers – first as settlers, at times consigning timber from their land as it was cleared for pasture, and then as pastoral or cropping farmers. For many decades these landholders used the railway for bringing in sheep and cattle to stock their farms, dispatching them to freezing works or, in the case of hill country holdings, for fattening on the lowlands. Lime and fertiliser came to the nearest railway station, as did fencing wire and later posts and gates. The mail, newspapers, groceries and general supplies came to the farmer's nearest town: in some areas the train brought these everyday needs to the nearest station, or a farm gate where the farmer picked them up from a train. Wool, grains and other produce moved on the train to processing plants or stores.

And, as described in The People's Railway, the farmer and the farming family looked to the train for transport to town, stock sales and other significant events. It was, for all those within reach of the railway, the transport lifeline.

Better roads and the increasing volume of trucks and cars began to change this pattern from the 1920s onward. Rail passenger services were withdrawn progressively from 1926, often being replaced by a Railways Road Services bus or, in some areas, a private bus operator. Freight traffic remained with the railways in reasonable quantities until the 1960s, helped to some degree by the transport licensing legislation which restricted competition from road transport. This changed in 1961 when restrictions on the movement of livestock disappeared. The rest is history, as set out in the introduction to this book.

The New Zealand farmer in 2004 rarely has a direct association with the network railway operator. In some regions fertiliser is brought to a central depot by rail, but a local transport operator will bring it to the farm and often spread it. Wool, livestock and grain leave the farm by truck but will often move by rail from the freezing works, woolstore or flour mill, in a processed or, in the case of wool, compressed form – and in the case of export cargo, in a container packed and ready to ship.

The railway in rural areas is now an arterial route passing through farmland and towns that no longer have a station. It is, in a sense, a wholesale function: the old local, intimate, retail function has vanished, except with passenger services.

THE RURAL STATION

Achray

Achray, eight kilometres northwest of Culverden on the Waiau branch in North Canterbury, was typical of scores of tiny rural stations spread throughout the railway system to serve the needs of local landholders.

A small shelter shed, a single loop which, at capacity, would hold 20 18′ 6″ wagons, a loading bank which assisted farmers in transferring bagged fertiliser and grain, or loading wool bales: that was Achray. As with most small rural stations, freight traffic was concentrated around the harvest in January/March, the wool clip in spring and autumn and fertiliser in spring and autumn.

Passenger traffic was very light – the local area was not intensively settled. The shelter shed would, in early days, handle the occasional parcel or small consignment to or from a passing train, and contained boxes in which farmers could leave wagon orders or consignment notes for outward loads.

In the days before effective road transport – up to the 1920s – Achray would have had seasonal use on a moderate basis. But with improved roads and trucks, freight traffic was increasingly handled at Culverden, where wagon supply was more effective, and the goods shed provided security and shelter for small consignments of seed and other farming needs, which could be picked up by the farmer and his wife on their regular visits to town for shopping, stock sales and other business.

Achray became less and less used over the years, handling only a few tens of tonnes annually in its final years. But it had a curious institutional role which kept it open beyond its expected life. From 1936 to the mid-1980s railways were protected from road competition over certain distances. Achray, by its location and presence, prevented the unregulated movement of road freight between Christchurch and the northern areas of the West Coast via the Lewis Pass. Its presence as an 'open station' was mentioned in several transport licensing cases in the 1960s and '70s.

Achray disappeared when the Waiau branch was closed in January 1978.

Pullar, 1961

Pullar was one of six stations on the Waikaka branch, in Northern Southland. Opened in 1908, this was the classic rural branch line, carrying fertiliser and lime in for farmers, wool, livestock and grain outward. The branch was 21 kilometres long, running through fertile down country and mixed livestock/cropping farms. Gore, the regional centre, is 25 kilometres from Waikaka.

Pullar, like Achray, was another of the many very local stations on the original railway network. Here, it is a hot January day; the shelter shed, timber-fronted loading bank, stockyards and a solitary wagon (timber as well), which has brought bagged fertiliser for a local farmer, bask in the sun. The heavy canvas tarpaulin has been pushed over the side by the farmer; the guard, with help from the enginemen on the thrice-weekly train, will struggle to disentangle the ropes and fold it, to be returned to Gore or Invercargill in the guards van. The track on the siding is well shielded with rank grass: the weed-spray train has not been over it for a long time. Above the light rail, elderly sleepers and fine ballast of the main line runs the ubiquitous two-wire telegraph line, linking the branch by voice to Train Control in Invercargill.

The line closed 18 months later, in September 1962.

Pahia, Southland, 1964

There was a small dairy factory at Pahia, seen here behind the shelter shed. Cream was carried by the Tuatapere branch train from stations along the line and left on the cream stand to be picked up by the dairy company. The cans were returned, empty, the next day.

Local cartage of cream by rail was widespread until the early 1960s. It moved from stations such as Rotherham, in North Canterbury, to Christchurch; from near Inchbonnie, on the Midland line, to Hokitika; in North Auckland and in many other parts of the country. In some ways it typified the all-purpose railway, a small consignment, seasonal, not easy to handle – but the railway would look after it, and did. And the guard on such trains needed a strong back.

Whitecliffs, 1959

The Whitecliffs branch left the Midland line at Darfield in mid-Canterbury. It was not just the classic rural branch line, serving essentially local farmers. This line had an industrial component, taking coal to a clay tile plant at Glentunnel and bringing out the finished product and coal (lignite) from local mines around Coalgate. It also carried sand for industrial use from Whitecliffs to factories near Christchurch, as well as the output from and supplies to local farms.

By 1959 there were but two return trains a week, carrying grain in season, a little wool and livestock, but mainly the traffic to and from Glentunnel.

Whitecliffs station was tucked into a terrace above the Horarata River. The yard design and structures had changed little over the years: the engine shed (occupied in 1959 by the Midland Motors bus which ran daily to and from Christchurch), locomotive water supply (which probably supplied the railway house in the background), stockyards, passenger shelter and, rather more unusually, the high-level loading bank from which the sand was loaded (and from which this photograph was taken in 1959).

The railway closed a few years later, in 1962; the Glentunnel works closed in 1965. There is still much to see of the railway at Whitecliffs (the engine shed and high-level bank were still there in 2003), and the formation is clearly evident around Glentunnel, where locals have developed a small but interesting heritage trail based on the area's industrial and transport history.

Taipuha, 1969

Taipuha is in North Auckland, 35 kilometres south of Whangarei. It was just a rural station – staffed for signalling purposes, a loop for crossing trains, a siding for local traffic and the usual station fittings and furniture.

The morning Westfield-Whangarei goods train is setting down a wagon-load of fertiliser for a local farmer. The relatively new diesel locomotive is much larger in profile than traditional rolling stock, hence the notice on the shed warning of tight clearances.

Taipuha station and yard, the wagons and probably this earlier model locomotive are now all history.

Waimate, May 1961

The railway reached Waimate in 1877. The main line between Timaru and Oamaru sensibly followed a direct route, without deviating to pass Waimate, situated near the entrance to the Waimate Gorge which gave access to the rich down country of the Waihao Downs and Waihaorunga areas.

Waimate goods yard, shown in this photograph, was on a spur at right angles to the original route, which continued through the Gorge to Waihao Downs until its closure in 1953.

The station was one of George Troup's more elaborate designs. (It was he who designed our most elaborate station, at Dunedin). The mock-Tudor finish and Marseille tiles were features of this general design which appeared at stations such as Dannevirke, Blenheim, Picton and Temuka. Only Blenheim survives in unmodified form; others, less elaborate, have been or are being restored at Mataura and Oamaru.

Scheduled rail passenger traffic to and from Waimate ceased in 1931. The ubiquitous Railways Road Services buses served the town from then on, both on trunk routes and with the Monday-Saturday local bus service to meet the South Island Limited express at Studholme.

The station in 1961 had sat unused for many years, apart from short-term storage. In the final years of its life the canopy provided storage for some of the local potato crop, a significant element in the branch line's traffic until it closed in 1966.

The goods shed, however, and the attached goods office were busy until the line closed. Every afternoon Monday to Friday, the Oamaru-Timaru local goods train paused at Studholme, collected traffic from Christchurch and north which it had left there that morning on the southbound trip, added the traffic from south and brought the lot to Waimate. In the early 1960s it would be anything from six to over 20 wagons per day: coal for the gasworks and domestic use, timber for building, cement, fertiliser, beer in barrels, and every day a large wagon full of general freight from Dunedin and a smaller wagon from Christchurch. And there were odd consignments from odd places – like the horse-drawn grader from Hawarden, North Canterbury.

The yard was busy at the harvest, January to March. All grain (mainly wheat) was bagged; the first bulk wheat was dispatched in 1961. Every wagon available was loaded with grain. Then in May the potato traffic began, mainly to the ports at Timaru and Oamaru for shipment to the North Island.

The freight yard and goods shed were the general freight focus for the town. Two staff were kept busy looking after customers and the associated paperwork. But with large trucks, better roads, concentration of distribution in larger centres and other factors, Waimate's rail traffic declined – just as changing methods of farm production, particularly bulk handling, diminished the role of the local railway station.

Alexandra, January 1980

Every January for many years train operations on the Otago Central branch were dominated by the 'fruit trains': special services bringing the Central stone fruit crop from stations between Alexandra and Cromwell to Dunedin and points beyond. In latter years fruit loading was concentrated at Alexandra, with handling made more efficient by the use of pallets. Prior to that every case was individually handled.

Here, on 22 January 1980, the district's fruit growers gather at Alexandra freight yard for their product to be put on pallets, sorted and placed in the wagons seen in the background. The special train would travel to Dunedin that night, and fruit for further north, including the North Island, would be quickly dispatched north on an express service.

This was one of the last years that the fruit crop moved by rail. Similar services ran on the Roxburgh branch until the mid-1960s.

STORES AND SIDINGS

To provide the linkage between rural stations and stores or processing plants, farm services companies had two options: to locate in or close to the railway yard, or to build a connecting track from the main line to the plant or store.

Both practices were widespread, especially in the South Island where grain and seed stores were widely distributed to meet local needs. A few examples follow.

Balfour, 1968

Balfour, in Central Southland, was in the heart of a rich mixed livestock/cropping area, and the stock and station agencies of the time were well represented in the township. Two of the major companies were located in the railway yard or on its boundary. It was a logical decision: the railway station had long been the freight transport hub in the town, and many farmers would call on visits to town to pick up materials for their farm. Wright Stephenson's added to the site advantage by having its own railway siding, which enabled consignments of grain and seed to be handled directly to and from its store.

The line from Lumsden to Balfour closed in 1978; the rest of the line, to Gore, had closed in 1971.

East Gore, 2001

The names on the stores have changed but the function is still the same. As late as 2001 there was still a working siding into these stores, at the north end of Gore. The main traffic was outward consignments of grain; the motive power for shunting within the siding was an elderly tractor with a large buffer, seen on the grass in this photograph.

The Wool Store, Timaru

Timaru had a line of wool and grain stores to both north and south of the railway station, and even behind the south end of the station. Most have closed; none now have direct rail access. But in 1998 the tracks were still down in this wool store, linked to the main sidings by a now abandoned wagon turntable.

Ashburton, 1976 and 1986

If a store was placed in a position where the permissible curve radius could not be achieved, the answer to the access problem was – install a wagon turntable. There were scores of these turntables throughout the South Island, serving stores, timber yards and other industrial sites. It was essentially a southern feature: there were very few in the North Island.

Ashburton had half-a-dozen turntables; most, such as that shown in the first photograph, were removed in yard rationalisation projects in the 1970s and 1980s. The last in service in the country was at Canterbury Roller Flour Mills at the north end of the Ashburton railway yards. The tractor is about to propel the wagon across the busy main road in November 1986. The wagon would be loaded in the mill with bagged flour for the North Island. The siding closed in the early 1990s; as the four-wheeled wagons were withdrawn the turntables could not be used. And crossing what was to become State Highway One became increasingly hazardous. Bagged flour is now loaded into containers on trucks and for long hauls is transferred to rail at the local container terminal.

J & T Meek's Mill, Oamaru, 1980

The same subject again, but inside the flour mill's premises. The hoses for bulk flour loading and the weighbridge are on the main siding, but the turntable was there for access into the building. The turntable is an old and short one, designed to handle wagons that were largely out of service by 1980. Its main role would have been to handle inward loads of bagged wheat from local stations and get them into the storage area inside the mill.

Harraway's Mill, 1980

This mill is located at Green Island, just south of Dunedin. The railway connection was of long standing, but it was to cease shortly after this photograph was taken in January 1980. Again, distribution methods changed, with bulk flour carried in special containers and the finished product loaded in ordinary containers and transferred to rail in Dunedin. Wheat was, at this stage, brought in by road.

Gear Meat Company, Petone, 1964

Freezing works were traditionally sited close to the railway network, both for incoming livestock and transfer of the product – and by-product – to ships' side or the domestic market.

The size and scale of many works called for extensive railway networks within their site boundaries. All had small locomotives, or road tractors, to move wagons around their sites. Some had virtual branch lines to link their sites with the main line: the Gear Meat Company at Petone was an example. Two tracks ran for about a kilometre next to The Esplanade, with a siding crossing the road to the Odlin's timber plant and several tracks crossing the road to various parts of the freezing works. Another track left the main line just south of Petone station and crossed Hutt Road to serve the works' extensive stock yards. Each morning, in the mid-50s, several long rakes of loaded sheep wagons would be waiting in Petone goods yard to be shunted down the track for unloading.

The photograph shows the small ex-NZR steam locomotive shunting on The Esplanade, with insulated wagons (loaded with meat) about to be propelled to the exchange sidings by the main line south of the Petone overbridge.

The works, and the railway, finally closed in 1982. So ended a railway route which, built in 1885, had once extended along the Petone foreshore as far as Hutt Park.

RAILWAYS AND LIVESTOCK

Addington, May 1961

Livestock traffic was, until the early 1960s, a significant traffic on New Zealand Railways. It fairly reflected the role of (mainly) cattle and sheep in the rural economy with over 8,000,000 head of sheep and 800,000 head of cattle being carried in the year to March 1960. There was also significant calf and pig traffic.

Cities and regional centres all had major saleyards, with a day or two scheduled each week for particular classes of stock, according to the season. Few saleyards could rival the size and scale of activity of Addington, the saleyards in Christchurch, which handled stock from as far away as Marlborough, South Canterbury and the West Coast.

Given this hinterland, it was no surprise that the railways had a major role in servicing Addington, both for incoming consignments and for distribution of the sale's results. This stock, in turn, could go all over the South Island.

But the saleyards had an important local role as well, as the first photograph shows. A mix of farmers' trucks and the standard vehicles in use by commercial road transport until the late 1950s is lined up at the loading points. The trucks are tiny compared to the truck and trailer units of the 21st century; it is perhaps understandable that the railway could still compete with trucks of this size over relatively short distances. The lines of railway wagons at the rear right mark the equivalent loading points for rail.

The Molesworth Train, Addington, 1961

Molesworth, a high country sheep and cattle station in inland Marlborough, produced in its annual muster a line of cattle eagerly sought after at the Addington saleyards.

These cattle were, from 1957 until about 1970, driven on the hoof from Molesworth to the railhead at Culverden, then several trains brought them to Addington. In the last years of rail being used there were over 1000 head to move; this called for up to four trains, which in turn required at least one service to run two return trips. Many of the South Island fleet of cattle wagons were brought to Christchurch for this event.

The photograph shows a service of empty cattle wagons passing the rail loading races at Addington in 1961, on the way to Culverden for Molesworth cattle. It also shows the ability to load and discharge large numbers of livestock to and from railway wagons; the platforms and races extend almost the whole length of the saleyards.

The Stock Train, 1956

For many years after World War II Rotorua was the major loading point for sheep and cattle from the land development projects to the south of the city. Every summer stock specials ran from Rotorua to the large freezing works then located in the Auckland urban area at Westfield and Southdown.

Loads for northbound trains were severely limited by the Tarukenga Bank, between Ngongotaha and Mamaku, with a grade of 1:35. The locomotive on this train would have had a full load, almost all sheep, as it climbs the bank in February 1956.

Today, there is fewer stock (especially sheep) on the farms, and there are more local freezing works to process them. And it is all handled by road transport. *Derek Cross*

The Branch Train

The rural branch line was a feature of most regions in New Zealand. In the days of passenger traffic the local train, and often the men who worked on it, were a local institution. The branch line was especially significant in the South Island where Canterbury and Southland had many such rural lines. The main line south of Christchurch generally ran close to the coast, and the branch lines stretched inland toward and sometimes into the hill country behind the plains. In the North Island the main routes tended to pass more through the middle of the productive regions, with a lesser need for branch lines. Also, the North Island topography, and different farming patterns, made railway construction less attractive than on the plains of Canterbury and Southland.

At the peak of railway mileage (in 1953) there were 11 rural branch lines in Canterbury, seven in Otago and 10 in Southland, a total of 28. The North Island, by contrast, had only 12 lines that were rural based rather than industrial or coal lines.

Waimate, October 1961

The Waimate shunt picks up wagons from the loading banks at Waimate. The hand-wound crane was used to transfer loads such as steel from wagon to truck. It could handle up to four tons, with hard work from men on the big handles to lift and swing it. Such cranes were at a few stations into the late 1960s or even 1970s; a very few are preserved now at heritage sites.

Over the road behind the freight yard is Waimate Transport Ltd's depot. Trucks at this time were typically 2 or 3-axle, mainly Bedfords, with a few 2-axle trailers. Some stock trucks were articulated, but still only 3-axle. Proximity to 'rail', as it was called, was important for the rural freight operator in those days. In most rural centres the two forms of transport worked together, and neighbouring sites helped that process.

The wagons to the right, with heavy standard black canvas tarpaulins, contained bagged fertiliser, mainly superphosphate, from the Ravensbourne plant near Dunedin. The advent of fertiliser handled in bulk on a serious scale was still some years away.

The farmer, or transport company drivers, would transfer the bags by sack, barrow or just muscle from wagon to truck tray, then again into the farmer's store or one of the stock and station agencies' stores in Waimate. There would often be consignments in the one wagon for several farmers or stores to give a worthwhile wagon-load of 8-12 tons.

Waikari, mid-1950s

The Waiau branch, from the junction at Waipara in North Canterbury to Waiau at the head of the Amuri Basin, served some of the most productive pastoral and arable land in inland Canterbury. This was reflected in the steady traffic on this line until the 1970s and the four staffed stations over the line's 66 kilometres – Waikari, Hawarden, Culverden and Waiau. For a station to be staffed other than for signalling there had to be a significant customer base and traffic flow, and this was the case through much of the branch's 59-year life. There were, at various stages, not only farm produce (especially livestock and grain) and fertiliser, but significant flows of timber, lime, flour and crushed stone for building blocks manufactured at Hornby, near Christchurch. Even honey was important for some years.

Waikari, the local commercial and distribution centre, received a steady flow of fertiliser and general goods from Christchurch. The small flour mill in the background provided steady traffic, and a limeworks loaded out to stations on the Canterbury Plains. The branch train would typically carry livestock, wool and grain (to other mills), along with small quantities of cream from Rotherham.

Some of this traffic is shown in this photograph of a typical Christchurch-bound train in the mid-1950s. There was a short steep climb from Waikari station to the top of the Weka Pass, a kilometre away, then a steady drift down the Pass, across the plains to

the junction with the main line at Waipara. Today the Weka Pass Railway operates from Waipara to the new Waikari station at the top of the Pass, with regular passenger services and the occasional mixed (freight and passenger) train, shorter but otherwise with similar rolling stock to that on the train in the photograph. *Derek Cross*

The Shunt, Pahiatua, late 1950s

Trains to service local stations ran regularly from railway terminals or junctions. These 'shunts', as they were called, were equivalent to a large-scale local carrier, moving between main line trains which could maintain faster schedules because the shunt looked after the local work.

The service in the photograph would probably have originated in Woodville, the then busy junction of the Palmerston North-Gisborne and Wairarapa lines. The shunt would service Pahiatua and intermediate stations to and from Woodville; it could go on to shunt smaller stations toward Masterton as required. The consist is mainly farmers' traffic – fertiliser, cattle wagons, a load of coal for a local merchant and an insulated wagon, probably for a local dairy company. *Derek Cross*

The Rural Railway

The illustrations, and the commentaries, have painted a picture of significant change in the rural sector over the last five decades. In few activities has the change been as significant as in transport, with the move from rail as the major supplier to rural areas to a point where there is now no direct contact with rural dwellers except as an arterial neighbour.

The visual impact of this change has been considerable. Perhaps, in a symbolic way, the December 1968 photograph of the Seaward Bush branch in eastern Southland, nearly two years after its formal closure in April 1966, makes the point. The line is redundant and in the process of demolition. The trains must stop, but the surrounding countryside and its economy carry on as before.

Chapter Three

THE MINERS' RAILWAY

Railways and coal mines have been inextricably linked in New Zealand's history. Even where a coal mine was remote from the national rail network, it was likely to have an internal railway system for bringing coal to the surface, or a private railway linking the mine to a port or to the main railway.

The selection of photographs which follows concentrates on the West Coast of the South Island. There have been – and still are – major coal fields in the Waikato, based around Huntly, and Southland, centred on Ohai. There is a belt of lignite deposits in the Canterbury and North Otago foothills; extraction has taken place near Coalgate, in the Mt Somers valley, at Ngapara and near Wedderburn, for example. And there are huge areas of lignite in Central Otago, central Southland, and other types of coal in inland Taranaki near Ohura and out toward the east coast of north Taranaki.

These photographs are about the structures and landscapes near where the coal was extracted, not so much about the mines themselves. Few of those scenes still exist, except in an abandoned form; some were semi-derelict when the photographs were taken.

The railway was a critical element in the distribution of coal – to a port, to the ultimate industrial or commercial consumer. It is the link to rail, large and small, which is the theme for this section.

Blackball, West Coast, 1960

Blackball lies in the foothills at the south-eastern end of the Paparoa Range, 28 kilometres by rail from Greymouth. The mine of the same name was long established, with extensive underground workings. The township, where many of the miners lived, was close by. The mine closed in the 1964 and the railway in February 1966, the latter prompted not only by the reduced output from the mine, but by the combined road-rail bridge across the Grey River at Ngahere being damaged by a major flood.

The photograph, taken in August 1960, is a classic West Coast mining scene. The bins, within which the coal was cleaned (of stone) and screened to various grades according to customer needs, dominates the valley. The mine mouth was to the left, and coal was brought to the top of the bins via the covered structure over the railway. The buildings included workshops, bathhouse, the administration buildings and others to serve the many needs of a significant mine and its staff.

The railway from Ngahere, the junction on the Stillwater-Westport line, climbed steeply (at 1:40) and with many sharp curves out of the Grey Valley to reach Blackball: it can be seen passing beneath the covered way leading from the mine and to the bins. The station yard was around the corner beyond the bins.

The Blackball mine produced bituminous coal, largely for industrial use. Over the years much was railed to Greymouth for transhipping to colliers, bound for North Island ports. This was a declining market in the 1960s, and the mine was increasingly expensive to work – hence the closure in the mid-1960s. The township remains, reduced in size.

Roa, August 1960

Coal from the Paparoa Mine had properties that made it attractive for processing to metallurgical coke and tar. This was carried out for many years at a plant at Sockburn, south of Christchurch. With changing markets, the plant closed in 1962 and the Paparoa Mine closed the same year. In more recent times new markets have been developed for this coal.

The railway from Blackball to Roa was unusual in various ways. It was owned by the Mines Department but was operated by the Railways Department. It was steep – 1:25 for nearly three kilometres, with some tight curves. Like the Dunollie-Rewanui section closer to Greymouth, it had centre rail braking, which called for special vans on the coal trains. Opened in 1909, the line closed (from Blackball to Roa) in July 1960, and coal was trucked to Blackball for loading on rail.

The photograph below shows the coal dump at Roa with the small rail loading yard.

Coal Bins, West Coast

Bins were, for almost all coal mines, an essential feature of the production process – for storage, cleaning and screening. These structures took many forms, designs and scales. The photographs which follow show a selection of these structures, all linked to the railway network and variously supplied by ropeway, narrow gauge railways, flume, aerial ropeway or truck.

Granity, 1978

Granity, 28 kilometres from Westport, once handled coal from mines in the Stockton area, on the plateau behind the narrow coastal strip north of Westport. Originally, an aerial cableway had brought the coal down to the coast. That had closed in the late 1960s, and in the last years of the original mines on the plateau the coal was trucked to Granity.

The timber-framed bins were large by local standards. They have since been demolished, the ropeway to Ngakawau (two kilometres north of Granity) built, the Stockton mine redeveloped to supply export markets, and all coal handling to rail is now done at Ngakawau.

The Co-op Mines – Photographs on facing page at top

There have many smaller or private mines on the West Coast, known as co-op mines (reflecting the cooperative structure of their ownership). Their bins were on a smaller scale: some examples are shown in the next photographs.

Facing page upper left: Rewanui Yard, 1975. These timber bins were supplied by flume – that is, the coal was carried by water along the bridge behind the bins. The water was drained by the flume at the front of the bin and the coal loaded into wagons beneath the bin.
Facing page upper right: Rewanui Incline. When space was tight, unusual measures had to be taken to get coal into railway wagons. This co-op mine's bins were tucked into the

hill next to the steeply graded railway between Dunollie and Rewanui. The descending train stopped with empty wagons beneath the discharge point, the coal was loaded and the train proceeded to Greymouth. As the track was a grade of about 1:30, good train handling was needed to position the wagons.

The steep four-kilometre section of the Rewanui branch originally had a centre rail for braking purposes, but with more sophisticated train braking the centre rail was removed in 1965. The line closed in 1985.

Rewanui, 1982

Another co-op mine near the main coal-loading area for the Liverpool Mine at Rewanui: this co-op mine bin, on its own siding, was unusual in that it was built of steel. Like others in the area, this was flume fed and seemingly derelict when the photograph was taken in 1982, but the track was still in use.

Charming Creek Bins, 1959

This was the coal-handling base for the Charming Creek Coal Company, which operated in the area above the Ngakawau River gorge from 1930 to 1958. Other small mines and a sawmill also used the line, and the tracks were close to others that took coal out to Mokihinui Mine, in the valley above Seddonville.

Coal from the mines was brought down through the very rugged gorge on a light railway, complete with suspension bridge, tunnel and a wooden centre rail for braking purposes. The company rolling stock – small wagons – was emptied into the upper level of the bins and screened, and the coal was then loaded out onto trucks, or into NZR wagons that had come up the one-kilometre siding from Ngakawau station. The locomotive in the picture would have been used on that shuttle. Smaller and lighter diesel locomotives were used on the coal line, with its lighter track and weight limit on the suspension bridge.

This site, a year after the mine closed, was an industrial archeologist's dream. Apart from the locomotive in the photograph, there were the remains of at least two other steam locos over banks or buried in the nearby bush, plus sundry other items of rolling stock and equipment.

Today, the site has been tidied, and the route up the gorge has become a magnificent walkway, now managed by the Department of Conservation. Large sections of the original track – including some of the old centre rail – have been left in situ, as a practical

reminder of why the formation is there. Examples of rolling stock, a small locomotive and good interpretive signage explain the area's history, quite apart from the points of archeological and ecological interest along the river. This combination of natural and man-made features make the Charming Creek Walkway one of New Zealand's most varied and interesting.

Runanga Coal Siding, 1965

The towns of Runanga and Dunollie lie at the foot of the Paparoa Range, some eight kilometres from Greymouth. Many of the residents work, or have worked, at coal mines in the area. Liverpool and Strongman were two of the most notable mines in recent times (both are now closed), and there were many smaller mines, mostly co-op ventures, both in the same area or tucked away up the valleys off the Coast Road.

Not unnaturally, coal was the major fuel for home heating, and for many years for cooking. It was supplied by the Mines Department (the then owners of the larger mines), railed to a siding at Runanga and placed over the loading bay shown in the photograph. The wagons carried about six tonnes, which was discharged onto a truck and delivered to miners' households in the two towns. One tonne a month was supplied free: this was dumped on the street frontage, a practice still followed today.

The wagons would have travelled about eight kilometres from the Liverpool Mine, or from the James Mine. Only rail could be used from Rewanui as there was no road access to the mines.

The railway on the West Coast played a significant role in local transport services well into the 1960s. This was but one example of its close links to nearby communities. The distribution of coal to miners still takes place, although by road and with reduced amounts supplied.

COAL TRAINS

Near Seddonville, 1977

The railway that now terminates at Ngakawau, where export coal is loaded for dispatch to Lyttelton, used to run to Mokihinui Mine, 18 kilometres up the coast and then inland up the Mokihinui River. The section from Seddonville to Mokihinui Mine was closed in March 1974, and the track from Seddonville to Ngakawau was closed in May 1987. Mines had closed, or reduced output, and there was little other traffic.

The route above the river provided just enough space for a narrow road and the railway. The photograph shows the shunt from Seddonville with its daily load, heading back to Ngakawau and Westport.

Kaitangata, 1961

The Kaitangata Railway & Coal Company opened its mine and railway in 1876. The main line from Dunedin was opened to the north bank of the Clutha River in September 1875, and the rail connection (at Stirling) was thus completed.

There were several mines in the Kaitangata area, but the worn condition of the track and low output from the field were not enough to justify keeping the railway open after 1970. Coal was then loaded on rail at Stirling until it transferred to road transport in the 1980s, following deregulation of transport. Most was destined for Dunedin, only 80 kilometres away.

The coal company took its railway responsibilities seriously, providing not only the track but also a proper railway station at Kaitangata, its own guards van, its own locomotives (one of which survives at Shantytown, near Greymouth) and infrastructure such as engine sheds and wagon weighbridge. When the Mines Department took over control of the line in 1956, it maintained these features until the line closed.

Makareao, North Otago, 1980

It is rare to be able to fit a whole branch line into one photograph, but the Makareao branch, in North Otago, allows it to happen. From the hill above the terminus the line runs out across the Shag River valley to its junction with the now closed Dunback branch at Inch Valley, against the hills in the distance.

The Makareao branch was a spur, just four kilometres long, built to serve a limestone quarry and lime processing plant owned by Millburn Lime and Cement Company. In earlier days there were lime-burning kilns and crushers at the line's terminus, with tracks running at various levels to load out the product. In later years the plant was abandoned and an aerial cableway built from a quarry far above the railhead to bring limestone rock down to wagons. This was then taken to Burnside, south of Dunedin, as a basis for cement manufacture. The cement works closed in 1989 after major dam

construction projects had finished, and the Makareao branch had no good reason to remain open. It closed in June that year.

The wagons in this photograph are parked over the summer break ready to be hauled to Dunedin when cement production began again. The five days a week Makareao to Burnside 'Stone Train', as it was known, was a regular feature of Otago's railway scene for many years.

Not quite a mine, but close to it!

Mines: The Small Railways

Old Rewanui

Tucked away in the hills above Rewanui and the Liverpool Mine are the remnants of a township – sometime home to miners and other mine workers who lived in this isolated settlement until moving down to Runanga or other local towns. Most had left the old town by the 1950s. There was no road access from Dunollie to Rewanui, except by motor cycle alongside the railway. Regular trains ran to and from Greymouth and Rewanui until about 1984 to take mine staff to and from work.

The old town was linked to Rewanui by a rough track and a 600mm gauge railway, as seen here, slowly being covered with bush. A flume brings water down to Rewanui.

Behind Denniston, early 1970s

The 610mm gauge railway, either as a ropeway (jig line) or, around the bins processing area, just as an ordinary small railway, was a normal part of the underground mining scene. The mine has closed, the tubs and equipment abandoned in the photograph taken in the area behind Denniston.

Chapter Four

THE PEOPLE'S RAILWAY

For close to a century the railway was the major means of travel over any distance within New Zealand. Even for local or short-distance travel the railway dominated until the 1920s, when the impact of the private car and commercial bus services began to be felt. The result was from then on a progressive withdrawal of rail passenger services from branch lines, and then from main lines, until the last such local operations ceased in the 1970s (except for commuter trains in the Wairarapa and from Wellington to Palmerston North). Rail passenger services were, to city dwellers - the majority of New Zealand's population - the main line and provincial expresses, or local and suburban trains.

Perhaps it is worth going back to the first half of the 20th century, to obtain a picture of the importance of rail passenger services at the time – and to fully appreciate the state of change well under way by 1950.

To a rural-based economy, transport assumed pride of place in the range of rural services, and in the early 20th century no form of transport was so quick, reliable and cheap as the railway. The railway station became the central point for a town or district's commercial activities – and it was not without its social values either. The station signified the link with the world beyond the local community, whether it be a village or sizeable market town. Near the station would be the hotels, stables and shops placed to capture custom from the trains and to be close to the arrival point of their wares. Take early Gore, Palmerston North, Ohakune Junction: no 19th century main street could fairly be complete without the station, if not taking up one side of the road, at least not more than a block or so distant from the town's commercial centre. There were relatively few exceptions to this general rule. John A. Lee makes the point about Riversdale, the central Southland town where he spent some of his childhood:

> "Riversdale was, and still is, a one street village, with shops on one side of the street and the railway station on the other." (*Children of the Poor*, London Boston Edition 1963 pp 24-25)

The comparable settlement in other parts of New Zealand would have included variations on the theme. Perhaps a sawmill in the North Island, a dairy factory in Taranaki or the Waikato, a school, post office, bank, a lodge building and, in the bigger towns, a town hall and borough or county offices. It would be a close-knit community, there to serve the needs of local farmers, sawmillers or miners and those people in the town who provided services to those industries. The demand on services was relatively simple: food, clothing, shoeing of horses and repair of farm equipment, the provision of halls for social events and churches for worship. There was little call to move beyond the local district boundaries for the necessities of life. For that reason a visit to 'town' was a relatively rare, and therefore important, event. And the means of making this visit, the ride on the train, was regarded with equal solemnity, respect or disdain, according to one's age and the frequency of such visits.

This pattern of life, with its regional variations, was by no means peculiar to the town situated on a rural branch line. The round of life in such a settlement was much the same as the equivalent community elsewhere, but the attitudes toward the railway service were different.

A rural branch line was regarded as very much the property of the district's residents, an attitude which became even more marked if a line ran into an area in which roads were poor. Events in local history could generate a certain following in the community. Residents who had fought long and hard for a branch line, and succeeded, were brought closer by their common opposition or at least scepticism about the mysterious and remote 'them' of central government.

The branch line trains had a different 'style' from the main line services. The branch train usually ran a daily weekday return service to the regional centre: it was the community's link with the outside world in the days before widespread use of cars or telephones. The trains were worked by local men who often, after years of residence in the same town, became very much part of the local community. There are many tales of the train crew shopping for their neighbours when they were 'in town'. In short, the branch line and its train belonged; it was an institution, fought for, often abused, taken for granted, but in times of threats from outside, fiercely protected.

The arrival of the train from town was an event and probably one of the few breaks in the tedium of small-town life. John A. Lee again, on Riversdale:

> "The social events of the day were the daily arrival of the railways train with its delivery of mail, the synchronised departure of the mail coach to Waikaia ..."

or on the Motuhora Branch in the 1920s:

> "The mixed train went down [to Gisborne] in the morning, and returned in the evening with passengers, stores and mails from Gisborne. Its arrival was one of the highlights of community life in the small settlement.
> "Swinging hurricane lamps as they came down bush tracks, people walked from near and far to meet the evening train, often late because of the steep gradient between Waikohu and Matawai. While waiting for the train on cold winter nights they gathered around a fire in the station building and exchanged the gossip of the day. To them, the railway was the lifeline of the community." (*Gisborne Herald* 25 March 1959; part of a series of articles on the Moutohora branch at the time of the closure.)

The lifeline worked in other ways too:

> "The small smoking cars on railway branch lines were often fully occupied with commercial travellers, and especially so when the auctioneers and assistants of many mercantile firms

were passengers. It took anything from two to five hours to get to one's destination by slow trains, often engaging in shunting at intermediate stations ..." (*Southland Times* 1 July 1962 in which an Invercargill man recounted his experiences in Southland in the 1920s.)

It was not hard to hear in the protests about branch line closures in the 1950s and '60s the voices and memories of the people whose youth was intimately associated with their local line and its trains. These people will reminisce, in an inevitably favourable or entertaining light, about the train and the many incidents surrounding it. These are the same people who witness the withdrawal of other services from their rural towns and feel the discomfort of change. The folklore of the rural branch line is thus defined and set with an era.

The photographs that follow portray a small selection of events in and around the people's railway. As with the background notes, a few precede the period on which this book concentrates. Most bear witness to an era of local involvement by and with the railway which is now long since passed.

Motuhora, 1917

The railway had just reached Motuhora (to become Moutohora in 1951). The station and other buildings, in pristine condition, stand in sharp contrast to the island of freshly cut bush into which the railway has intruded. Given the unusual number of passenger carriages at the station, this may well have been opening day for the branch. It was a classic situation of a railway being built to 'open up the country' – the developmental role clearly assigned to railway construction at the time.

In the introduction to this section there is a quotation describing the role of the railway in a carless community. This is the setting for that quote. The railway lasted until 1959, by which time the cutover bush, and standing bush, had all been felled and cleared to make way for pasture. In 2004 one must look hard to see any physical trace of the railway that served this remote area, and its population, for 42 years. *Archives New Zealand, New Zealand Railways collection; Archives Ref: AAVK W3493, E5302*

Methven, c1907

Methven was the terminus of the 36-kilometre Rakaia-Methven branch, built by the Rakaia and Ashburton Forks Railway Co Ltd and operated for them by the Railways Department from December 1880. It was taken over by the NZR in April 1885 and served the rural farmland in the area until its closure in 1976. Passenger services were discontinued from September 1958.

The scene shows passengers from the train walking toward Methven township, about 200 metres away. Methven was busy enough to need a stationmaster and station building to match, although not as tall as the photo would suggest. The engine shed is immediately behind it; railwaymen's cottages are on the left.

Perhaps it was a special event, or the day of the week when people from stations along the line regularly came to town for shopping. Some of the people near the station would be there to greet visitors. The scene is a reminder of the importance of the train for all travel, including for relatively short distances, in the era before the private car or local bus service. *Archives New Zealand, New Zealand Railways collection; Archives Ref: AAVK W3493, E4866*

Hawkins, 1946

The mixed train (passenger carriages and freight wagons on the same service) or a refinement, the goods with car when there were few passengers, supplied the majority of local passenger services in rural areas. A few branch lines offered a one-day-a-week passenger service which was not delayed by the need to shunt freight. However, for most lines, especially in areas of sparse population, the train such as that shown in the photograph looked after both freight and passenger needs in the most economical way

– even if the passengers experienced very slow journey times, with waits at stations while the train shunted.

Hawkins was on the 18-kilometre Darfield-Whitecliffs branch in mid-Canterbury, opened in 1875 and closed in 1962. Passenger services ceased in 1949, as a Midland Motors coach had for some time provided a daily service from Whitecliffs to Christchurch, a much more effective service than the twice-weekly goods with car.

Hawkins served local farms and their residents. The passengers are waiting for the car-van (a combined carriage/guards van with space for parcels and small freight) to draw up to the platform. They could be visiting friends or going to Coalgate, seven kilometres along the line, for shopping.

The box wagon next to the carriage would be a 'roadsider' wagon, carrying small consignments of freight to and from stations along the line. And in those days many guards vans carried a mail box in which people could place letters: it is situated in the car-van just ahead of the open freight door, beneath the handrail. Letters posted there would often carry a late fee of a few pence, but most train guards would willingly take mail into town for posting if the van box was not open. *Alan Bellamy*

Stratford, 1974

One of the last routes to carry passengers on mixed trains was the Stratford-Okahukura line, linking Taranaki and the North Island Main Trunk. The area traversed by this line is rugged, with steep hill country for much of the route. Roads were narrow and, in wet weather, unreliable. The railway, completed as recently as 1933, for many years provided passenger, freight, mail and newspaper delivery services to farms and villages along the line, especially in the central section between Douglas and Ohura. The main

road is distinguished as being one of the last sections of state highway to be sealed.

Many of the freight trains on this route had a passenger carriage attached; the last of these was withdrawn in 1978, as there was by then little demand from passengers. The photograph shows a goods with car in the freight yard at Stratford ready to leave for Taumarunui. It would be a long journey with frequent stops to put off the livestock wagons at stations along the line, to be reloaded and brought back to the freezing works at Waitara.

Huiroa, 1981

As passenger numbers on the Stratford-Okahukura line fell away in the 1960s/'70s, there was still a residual demand from people wishing to travel in reasonable comfort between the central North Island and Taranaki. The mixed train services could not supply any quality of service and were withdrawn in 1978. The daily New Plymouth-Auckland railcar service no longer ran over the route after 1971, and the railcars that had provided that service were worn out.

The Railways Department's response was to provide a daily New Plymouth-Taumarunui return passenger train service – usually a locomotive, guards van and

passenger carriage. There were still some mail and parcels to carry; passenger numbers were typically in the 15-30 range. The photograph shows the train near Huiroa in May 1981, two years before the service ceased in 1983.

Seddon, mid-1970s

Over the years since the Christchurch-Picton route was opened in 1945 there has been a variety of passenger services linking these two centres. Steam-hauled expresses a few days a week; a daily railcar service, introduced in 1956; diesel-hauled express trains in the 1970s; a short period with no passenger service; and now the Tranz Coastal, which runs from Christchurch to meet the Interislander ferry at Picton and returns in the afternoon. The latter service makes few stops along the route; the great majority of its custom is at Kaikoura, Blenheim and the two terminals.

Here the north-bound 1970s express has paused at Seddon, 25 kilometres south of Blenheim, to let off a few passengers. The guard in those pre-radio days is giving the right-away signal to the locomotive driver, and the longer-than-usual-train with its midsummer holiday passengers will head down to the double-decked bridge over the Awatere River, over the Dashwood Pass and on to Blenheim.

Riccarton, 1959

Christchurch at one stage had a range of suburban or local train services, linking the city to Rangiora, Lyttelton and Burnham. All have now been withdrawn, the last to go being a single return service on weekdays between the city and Rangiora, which ceased in 1976.

This service had a railway function as well as serving people who worked in the eastern sector of the city; Addington workshop staff who lived along the route were regular users. In 1959 there were still two return services daily. The photograph shows the first train of the afternoon approaching Riccarton railway station on its way to Rangiora. Riccarton at that time was a small but busy freight yard, handling coal consigned to local merchants who loaded it into sacks and delivered it to homes, as well as timber consigned from the West Coast, and wheat and flour traffic to and from the flour mill sited on what is now the grounds of Christchurch Girls' High School.

Khandallah, 1967

Khandallah and Ngaio were the only two stations between Wellington and Johnsonville when the Wellington and Manawatu Railway Company opened their railway between Wellington and Longburn (near Palmerston North) in 1886. Given the steep grades, which kept trains short by modern standards, and the frequency of trains, loops for trains to pass were needed at reasonably close intervals.

Khandallah, from its inception, had one of those loops, along with a siding for handling freight. Crossing loops are ideally close to level, and in order to allow trains longer than the short loop to cross, backshunts were added to each end of the loop. Hence the need for a signal box, from which the interlocked signals and points were operated to allow trains to work their way past each other on a busy line.

When the railway became the Johnsonville line after the North Island Main Trunk was diverted through the Tawa Flat tunnels in 1937, the freight siding was closed and a shelter shed and platform built on the loop, and Khandallah then existed only for passengers and parcels to and from the already well-settled and soon to be rapidly growing areas served by the station. The backshunts were kept for the possibility of a three-train crossing (there was still freight traffic to and from Johnsonville and Ngaio until about 1970). The signal box was needed to work the points and complex interlocking, should a crossing occur – but it rarely did, with most three-train crossings taking place at Ngaio.

The backshunts were removed in the 1970s. The only remnants are the formation at each end of the loop and the points at the north end of the loop which are still interlocked with the signalling system. The old station and signal box were demolished soon after this photo was taken in 1967.

Near Blenheim, 1956

For many years local passenger and mixed trains ran between larger towns and nearby centres in various parts of New Zealand. The miners' trains around Greymouth and Westport, and Invercargill-Bluff were examples. Some were frequent enough to be suburban services, others were one step back, 'local' trains, usually stopping at all stations along a relatively short route.

Blenheim and Picton were two centres linked by such services. That section of railway was opened in 1875, and the main line slowly extended south toward Christchurch until being linked to the rest of the South Island system in 1945. There were school trains (Queen Charlotte High School in Picton did not open until 1964) and boat trains to and from *Tamahine*, the ferry which ran several times a week between Picton and Wellington until superseded by the rail ferry *Aramoana* in 1962.

The trains were not big, as the numbers to be carried were a few hundred a day each way. The train shown here was typical of the local passenger services which plied this area and other parts of New Zealand until the post-World War II years, occasionally as mixed freight and passenger services. The Picton services lasted longer than many, being withdrawn in 1964. The 'boat trains' had ceased in 1958. *Derek Cross*

Auripo, Central Otago, 1968

The Otago Central branch to Cromwell had one of the last local rail passenger services in the country. The route had steam-hauled passenger and mixed trains, but from as early as 1938 there had been tentative plans to introduce railcars.

Agitation for improved services became more serious after World War II and continued with growing vigour until the first regular railcar service began in September 1956. It was suspended in autumn 1957 until November of that year while major track repairs were carried out. From May 1958 the railcars ran only to Alexandra, with Railways Road Services coaches providing links to Clyde, Cromwell and beyond.

Road routes to and within Central Otago did not always parallel the railway. Road access from the junction at Wingatui to Sutton (57 kilometres) was very difficult, although population density was very light. Again, a number of settlements (and stations) beyond Ranfurly to Alexandra were remote from the main road and a potential bus route, especially within Ida Valley.

Custom was not always good, except for the Sunday service between Dunedin and Alexandra, which was very popular. But while other routes had lost their local passenger services during the 1950s and '60s, the Otago Central railcar continued until April 1976.

The photograph shows the morning railcar from Alexandra picking up passengers at Auripo in the Ida Valley, one of the more isolated stations on the route. A local farmer and his family have come to the station in his farm truck. Both passenger and freight traffic at Auripo is light, the number of people do not justify a platform. For freight there is only a loading bank for wool and, behind the truck, yards and a race for loading sheep on to wagons. *George Emerson*

Lauder, 1976

For much of the year the Sunday afternoon railcar service from Central Otago operated in the dark, and by April the 5.40 pm Sunday service from Alexandra to Dunedin would be looking for passengers at stations in the gloom as it traversed the lightly populated areas along the route. This photograph was taken at Lauder on the final trip on Anzac Day 1976, by which time patronage had fallen to a level that could not justify the railcar's retention. For those on the main road there was a coach, but for most the private car provided the service they sought. *D.L.A. Turner*

Travellers' Havens

In the introduction to this section of the book there is mention of the services that in the 19th and early 20th centuries clustered around a town's railway station. Hotels and boarding houses (in effect private hotels without a licence to sell liquor) were often part of that cluster.

The two photographs show examples from each end of the scale. The Railway Hotel, opposite the railway station at Invercargill, is one of the grander examples of a hotel ideally sited to meet the needs of people travelling to and from Invercargill by train, especially commercial travellers with their cases of samples. It is still there, with a New Zealand Historic Places Trust rating.

The other example is at Rangataua, four kilometres south of Ohakune. Once the site of a major Railways works depot, and with two major sawmills nearby, there was a need for accommodation for men visiting these plants. Ruapehu House Private Hotel, situated just over the road from the station, was where they stayed. It was located in a dry area (no liquor could be sold there), hence the lack of a licensed hotel.

Ruapehu House was, in its latter years, a private home. It was demolished in the 1990s.

Ruapehu House, 1968

Railway Hotel, 1970s

The Kaikoura Trots Train, Riccarton, 1959

Racing and trotting club meetings were popular forms of recreation for many decades. Trains were the customary form of transport to such events held outside the main centres. For many years a special train ran from and to Christchurch for the October meeting of the Kaikoura Trotting Club. It conveyed not only people attending as patrons, but also horses, sulkies, trainers and jockeys.

Over the years the demand for the train and its various cargoes diminished. Horse floats carried the horses and trainers; other people went by car. And as a midweek meeting, it had a limited potential market.

The October 1959 train to Kaikoura, shown about 7.00 am passing at speed through Riccarton station, was one of the last to run. The consist includes three carriages, the obligatory guards van, a flat-deck wagon for sulkies, and two horse wagons, each capable of carrying four horses and their attendants.

The Picnic Train, Studholme, 1961

In the days before widespread ownership of cars, trains were extensively used for groups to travel to and from their annual picnic or indeed simply as an opportunity for getting out into the country. During summer for many decades Railways ran 'mystery trains' from Christchurch, with hundreds of people spending a Sunday at Oxford, Motukarara or other rural destinations where there was a suitable park or beach.

The tradition faded as more people began to own cars and branch lines closed; many of the most attractive destinations were on these lines. Excursions to main line centres, such as Caroline Bay (Timaru) or Kaikoura ran regularly from Christchurch until the early 1960s. And the Railways picnic was a well-established institution, running from centres with a significant New Zealand Railways staff to take their families for a day out. The Frankton Junction (Hamilton) picnic train to Mt Maunganui was a very significant event. At the other end of the scale, in the late 1940s the staff at Gisborne would go to Opoutama – a trip that included special Sunday trains on the Moutohora branch to Gisborne to bring staff and families to and from this important event.

This photograph shows one of the last of the Canterbury picnic trains – the Presbyterian parishes of Timaru returning from their day at Victoria Park in Waimate. It is late on a March Sunday in 1961, and the long train is drifting into Studholme (the junction with the main line) on the way home to Timaru, after a day of races, ice cream, fierce sunshine and companionship. The next morning the carriages would be returned to Christchurch, and the Waimate branch would relapse into its one return freight train a weekday routine.

Chapter Five

RAILWAY FURNITURE AND FITTINGS

To most people a railway is the track, the station and the trains. But there was a huge and varied collection of 'furniture and fittings' which made up the working railways, from the more obvious, such as water vats and goods sheds, to the less apparent, such as dog kennels and culverts.

The selection that follows is just that: a sample of the buildings and equipment found on the traditional railway. Few of these remain today: some have been relocated to heritage sites; most have been demolished.

THE RAILWAY STATION

There have been, over New Zealand's railway history, some 1300 railway stations. Almost all had a station building or a shelter shed, a few were just name boards, many were similar in the layout of their facilities – but few were exactly the same.

The three following examples could be fairly classed as classic rural stations.

Eketahuna, 1979

Eketahuna was in its final years as the railway centre for a large, mainly pastoral farming district when this photograph was taken. By 1979 livestock was being carried by road, and the limit for competition by road transport with general freight had been extended to 150 kilometres. Some fertiliser was still coming in by rail, some wool was going out; but much of the other traditional railway traffic was steadily transferring to road.

The Wairarapa line was still using the tablet system for train control, and the semaphore home signal, once a classic feature on many of the main and secondary routes, was still in use. The last of those signals went out of use some 20 years later. Beyond the level crossing lies all the standard furniture of a rural station: the stockyards, with the cattle yards having been rebuilt with railway irons (it had been a busy stock-loading station), the goods shed, a loading bank, a five-tonne capacity gantry crane and the large wooden station (replaced in the early 1980s with a small modern structure).

In 2004 only the concrete loading bank and the station platform edge remain; only the main line track is left.

Parnassus, 1970

Parnassus, in North Canterbury (*below left*), was the terminus of the line north from Christchurch from 1912 to 1939. When the line was extended to Hundalee in 1939 and finally opened to Picton in 1945, Parnassus became just the station for a significant farming hinterland and for a township providing rural services.

The painting team had just done their job when this photograph was taken. Apart from the usual features of the station building, goods shed and loading bank (the stockyards had already gone), the dominant feature is the water vat. A few of these stayed for a while after the withdrawal of steam locomotives (in 1971) to service local houses or provide water for the weed-killer train. There is also a good collection of the smaller buildings which seemed to sprout around stations of this size. The red ones at the foot of the tank are trolley sheds. The motorised "velocipedes" (in official terms) used by track staff were held there when not out on the track, and one other shed was used for holding track tools and equipment and possibly stocks of smaller track fittings. The green hut nearer the station would contain signalling equipment; beyond the station there was a men's toilet.

Little of these fittings remains in 2004; the main line is the only significant railway feature in Parnassus.

Owhiro, 1978

Owhiro (*above right*) was a flag station three kilometres south of Mosgiel, near Dunedin. In passenger terms it used to serve local farms; the last service scheduled to stop there ran in the mid-1950s. But the ubiquitous track telephone was in the station; hence it lasted another 40 years as a large telephone shelter, and was painted in the normal painting cycle. As track telephones became redundant in the 1990s with the advent of radios for train crews and track staff, so did the shelter shed, with its rare and elegant round-top door, become 'surplus to requirements'. It was destroyed by fire in about 1996.

Owhiro was, until the 1990s, a busy freight station. Lime from near Oamaru was unloaded there for distribution on the Taieri Plains, and a private siding to a large grain and seed store provided regular traffic until the mid-1990s.

STATION FURNITURE

The Men's Toilet, Matiere, 1986

Many stations, even the smaller ones where there was a modicum of passenger traffic, had men's toilets. They came in various sizes according to passenger numbers at the site. Matiere, 27 kilometres from Taumarunui on the line to Stratford, served a small township and an area of extensive pastoral farming. The station was staffed until about 1975. The toilet (*below left*), with two stalls and urinal, was in the classic form: timber frame on concrete, with corrugated iron cladding and the urinal unroofed.

By 1986, Matiere station had been closed, the township had virtually disappeared and the toilets remained for use by track and train staff.

Dog Kennels, Studholme, 1980

For many dog owners the traditional method of moving dogs around New Zealand was by train – in the 'dog boxes' which were part of most guards vans. Many of the boxes' occupants were farm dogs, moving to a new home after a sale or returning from a long droving task. Domestic dogs also moved around the country. For long journeys station staff watered the dogs at junctions or where there was a change of train, and at larger stations kennels were provided to hold them until their train came or until their owner came to pick them up.

The kennels at Studholme (*above right*, backing on to a large edition of the standard outdoor men's toilet) were little used by 1980. Farmers would usually drive to and from sales, carrying their dogs with them, as would the owners of domestic dogs. For long trips the dogs would fly, and by the early 1980s dogs rarely travelled by rail except by special arrangement, in a portable dog box in the guards van.

The Safe, Ohura, 1997

All 'officered' stations, that is those with a stationmaster, had a safe for holding cash from customers, pay for staff, and valuable documents. These safes were not only reasonably secure in their own right, but were set in a very solid concrete surround. They were designed to withstand fire, as well as theft.

As stations were closed, whether as a result of a line closure or the disappearance of a major traffic source, the station was usually sold for removal or demolished. The safe was the hard part of the demolition and, in the case of Ohura, it was left as a lonely sentinel at a once busy station, which had handled large quantities of coal from local mines and serviced the local farmers. Only the crossing loop and one siding remain from the many tracks once in the yard, together with, at least in 1997, the goods shed and remnants of the stockyards.

Another example of a lonely safe is on the site of the former Hunterville station, now a well-kept garden, thanks to the efforts of a local resident.

The Railway Gates, Cust, 2001

The Public Works Department, which built much of the railway network, had standard designs for most station and yard fittings. The gate, usually made from jarrah, and with either four or five bars, was an essential feature at any station where livestock was driven along roads, often to or from the station stockyards. Gates of this design were installed on the Rimutaka Deviation as late as the 1950s; it was a long-lasting design.

The gates at Cust in North Canterbury were photographed in 2001. Cust, one of the more significant stations on the Oxford branch, closed in 1959. The Waimakariri District Council has, in recent years, made a feature of remnants of the old line as part of a local heritage trail. Station signboards, goods sheds on farms and the cart and pedestrian gates at Cust, leading to a park on the old station site, are part of the trail. A photograph of Cust Station and yard is on page 91.

Railway Houses, Tahora, 1981

The railway house was a major feature of the railway landscape over the years. Its location ranged from the solitary home at a small station, to a large settlement such as those at Ngaio (Wellington) or Frankton Junction (Hamilton), which, with over 100 homes, had its own recreation, sport and social facilities. The Railways housing 'fleet' reached a maximum of some 6000 in the 1950s.

One reason for providing houses arose from the need to have staff in relatively remote locations, where there were few houses to buy or rent. Today, with improved transport, mechanized track maintenance, automatic signalling and little local traffic, that need has gone and so have the houses. In 2004 only one house remains in the railway's ownership, at Cass, in the South Island high country.

Tahora, about half way between Stratford and Okahukura was, and still is, remote. The houses in the photograph were built for track staff, on a then busy line running through rough country and calling for track staff along the route. There was little else there, apart from local farms.

The Track, Dunsandel, 1976

Railway track, and its formation, is not lightly called 'the permanent way'. Given good formation, ballast and maintenance, it will last for many decades.

Here, at Dunsandel in mid-Canterbury, on the siding serving the high-level loading bank used for loading grain and scrap onto wagons, is bull-headed rail from the days of Canterbury Provincial Railways. At the time of the photograph the rail would have been at least a century old. The track has 'chairs' supporting it rather than the modern method of plates and clips or bolts into the sleepers. The rail is locked into the chairs by wooden wedges. Examples of this old track structure lasted on sidings around Canterbury until into the 1990s.

The Trackman's Hut, Matarae

When track staff travelled on trolleys, huts were needed along the railway for shelter and for holding stocks of smaller track fittings. With the advent of, first, gang buses, then the hi-railer (a truck fitted to run on railway lines), such huts were no longer needed. Few survive today: these two photographs were taken on the Taieri Gorge Railway, near Matarae. On a heritage railway, such fittings still have a role.

Cattle Stop, Waikari, 1976

When stock droving was a regular practice, the railway line had to be protected from wandering livestock at level crossings. Hence, the standard 'cattle stop', even on sidings such as at the Waikari flour mill in North Canterbury.

The cattle stops began to disappear in the 1960s; today there are just a few left. The remainder will go as track is renewed or removed.

Culvert, Hyde, 1998

There would have been and still are thousands of culverts on the railway network carrying drains, small creeks and overflows beneath the railway formation. At Summit, on the Rimutaka Incline walkway, there are still the remnants of a timber box culvert, but more usually they were pipes (steel or concrete) or even built with dry stone walls.

In Central Otago, with its local supplies of stone, the stonemasons were called in to make probably the most ornate form of culvert facing in New Zealand. There are still many such examples on the Taieri Gorge Railway, inland from Dunedin, and indeed along the old railway formation from Middlemarch to Clyde, now the Otago Central Rail Trail. This one is at Hyde, beyond the end of the line at Middlemarch, but still with the railway station, yard tracks and some wagons on a privately owned site.

Samson Post, Fairton (near Ashburton), 1998

New Zealand's railways adapted British or American practices and designs as were appropriate. The British, in their designs for railway fittings and furniture, were thorough and their construction permanent. Their means of stopping wagons going off the track at the end of a siding were solid posts and a cross beam, designed to match the sprung buffers with which their stock is traditionally equipped.

New Zealand rolling stock did not have, apart from a few early examples, the twin buffers of British stock, nor did the local railway use the British simple chain and link coupling. The New Zealand 'chopper' coupling, still in use but in more robust form, was at the end of sprung drawgear and fulfilled the role of buffer and coupling in one.

The Samson post was expensive in materials and costly to install. Varieties of alternative buffer stops have been designed over the years, the more elaborate ones to protect assets behind them (such as in Wellington station platforms). But others have been simply piles of old ballast, sometimes contained in a concrete or timber 'fence' to stop the rubble spreading. They are cheaper, far less damaging to a wagon that might meet it at unseemly speed and more effective than the Samson post.

The post at Fairton is at the north end of the sidings serving the Fairton freezing works. It is one of very few that has lasted on a working siding. There are a few others (for example at Timaru) which no longer have track nearby.

Branch Line Locomotive Depot, Waimate, 1961

Waimate boasted an architecturally notable station, a significant goods yard and its own locomotive depot where, until the 1940s, a locomotive was based to operate daily to Studholme and, less frequently, out to 'The Downs'. As there was a water supply at the depot, the facilities were left in place for occasional use by locomotives there for longer than the usual one-hour visit from Studholme. The railway to Waihao Downs closed in 1953, to Waimate in 1966.

This scene was of the locomotive from a picnic train being watered. The crew's absorption in a distant scene is focused on a race in progress at the Waimate Racecourse.

The Rural Goods Shed, Parnassus

The simplest stations had just a siding for local traffic. A loading bank, and perhaps stockyards as yard 'furniture', were the next steps up; then the presence of a goods shed and perhaps a larger station building were the next signs of local significance.

There were, in 1957, some 260 goods sheds in the South Island alone. At least 200 of these were at stations that could fairly be described as rural, either in their role as local collection/distribution depots, or simply servicing local farmers. Parnassus, in North Canterbury, was firmly in the rural category, some 135 kilometres from Christchurch and 14 kilometres from Mina (the station for the rural service centre of Cheviot). This shed would have been used for holding less than wagon-loads of traffic for local farmers and sheltering wool brought to the stations from farms in several lots, and held until wagons were ordered or supplied. Rural communities relied on trust: freight rarely disappeared illicitly, even from unlocked sheds. And Parnassus, a staffed station until about 1970, had people on duty to keep an eye on local freight for much of the week.

The shed was a standard 31 x 21-foot design with a canopy to shelter freight being transferred between shed and wagon. Once a reasonably busy station, Parnassus has now closed as the trend toward all rural traffic moving by road, or via centralised freight depots, is completed. Few such buildings of the 200 plus (and an equivalent in the

North Island) remain in 2004, except by relocation to farms. With their departure, and the linked rural station closures, is a loss of intimacy between the railway and its local community – a move begun in the 1960s and completed in the 1980s with the deregulation of transport and the transfer of most rural traffic to road. Only fertiliser, and then in bulk to centralised depots, retains a tenuous link. Even by 1970 road haulage had made serious inroads into the shed traffic at Parnassus.

Waitaki Road Rail Bridge, 1955

The combined road-rail bridge was a feature of New Zealand transport infrastructure for many years. In most cases the construction of one bridge rather than two simply meant that the railway tracks were laid on the bridge deck, sometimes proud of the deck, sometimes with the deck built up to rail head. In a few cases, such as the bridges over the Awatere River just north of Seddon in Marlborough, and at Okahukura in the King Country, the bridge is double-deck, with the railway running above the road.

Many of these bridges were on lightly used railways and roads. Others were built on main roads, with busy railways, where wide river beds provided a problem. The braided beds of Canterbury's rivers were particularly challenging: the Rakaia, the two Rangitata bridges and, on the boundary with Otago, the Waitaki River, all had combined bridges well into the 20th century. The Rakaia rail bridge, at 1.75 kilometres, is the longest bridge on the network.

The last of these to be renewed was over the Waitaki River. The railway was opened in 1876, with road traffic using the railway bridge. A new road bridge was opened in June 1956, and a new railway bridge was built shortly afterwards. The photograph, taken through the windscreen of an Austin Somerset driving north in late 1955, shows clearly the rails sitting proud of the deck, and the need (as on most such bridges) to get one's car positioned correctly to avoid having to cross the rails.

Today, there are five single-deck combined bridges left: two are on the Taieri Gorge Railway, at Hindon (becoming a combined bridge only in recent years) and at Sutton. There are three on the national network, one over each of the Arahura and Taramakau Rivers, between Greymouth and Hokitika. Road traffic is heavy (it is a state highway), but rail traffic is usually just two trains a day. The last is at Pekatahi, between Edgecumbe and Taneatua in the Bay of Plenty. The railway line is at present unused but not formally closed.

Most of these bridges, including the five left in 2004, were only one vehicle wide. A few, such as the Waitaki, were busier and had two 'lanes', and had gates operated by bridge keepers who closed the bridge prior to train crossings. *W.J. Parr – supplied by Aidan Challis*

Locomotive, Ross, 1959

One of the endearing features of traditional sawmills and the areas in which they were located was a tendency to park equipment 'out the back' when its working life had finished. Today, scrap merchants and a general attitude of industrial tidiness have changed this convention. But in 1959 a former NZ Railways locomotive used by sawmillers Stuart & Chapman at Ross, in Westland, sat in the swamp behind the mill amongst other detritus from the mill. It continued to rust gently away over the decades and is reputed to be now buried on the site.

Perhaps not a working fitting, but a not untypical railway-flavoured scene near sawmills, and usually near the railway, on the West Coast and central North Island in the 1940s and '50s.

Chapter Six

THE LITTLE RAILWAYS

New Zealand has a rich history of 'little' railways – those built to link bush to sawmill, a local port to its immediate hinterland, a coalmine to the railway network. The stories of the bush tram have been well covered elsewhere; they would have been, in route distance, the most significant of the smaller railways. Some were long and busy enough to match or exceed tonnage levels on a rural branch line.

Many of the lines linking coal mines to ports, or the railways network, were equally busy. The Kaitangata Railway & Coal Company line in South Otago was one example; the Ohai Railway Board line from Wairio to Nightcaps still operates, but as part of the national system.

Then there were the truly little railways – the 600mm gauge jig lines with rope haulage, once a notable feature of the mines near Huntly, on the West Coast, in Southland and elsewhere. Thousands of skips or tubs brought coal from deep in the mine to the screens and bins, usually at a railhead. Tiny versions of these light railways serviced small private mines, with either ropes, manpower or horsepower.

Almost all the ropeways disappeared during the 1960s and '70s. Changes in coal extraction methods meant that flumes or large mechanical coal carriers were more efficient. More mining became opencast, with heavy diggers and trucks doing the extraction and transport. The ropeways and skips were sized for human involvement; modern mining is run to large-scale machine use.

This is equally the case with forestry. The bush trams were always a transitory mode as bush was cut out. They began to fade as stands became more remote, as the then Forest Service encouraged road construction so that forest management could be better practised, and logging trucks became larger and more efficient. The last of the bush trams, a few examples on the West Coast, closed in the 1960s. Indigenous timber extraction on any scale has now largely ceased; exotic timber extraction is via well-built forest roads leading to the national road network and a mill or port, or to a railhead from which train loads of logs are dispatched.

The photographs and commentary that follow show a few examples of these small railways in their last years.

The West Coast Bush Tram, Ruatapu, 1959

The West Coast of the South Island, with its extensive stands of indigenous timber, was home to a network of bush trams from the early days of sawmilling until the last working tram disappeared in 1967.

Butler Bros mill at Ruatapu, 18 kilometres south of Hokitika, was one of the biggest mills on the Coast and used bush trams until 1960. It was the last major tram operating on the Coast.

The bush 'lokey' at the skid site, where logs were loaded for transport to the mill at Ruatapu, about 16 kilometres away. This lokey (a name given to all bush tram locomotives) was an ingenious conversion/adaptation of steam to diesel, using the under frame and wheels of a steam locomotive with a new diesel motor and body. All work was done at Ross by Stuart & Chapman, another large mill with a skilled engineering workshop.

Behind the lokey is the log hauler, and on the hard right is the spar – a tall-standing tree, trimmed of its branches, which acts as the base for cables going out into the bush and bringing felled logs into the skids where they are loaded onto the tram bogies. This was known as the high-lead system and is still used in exotic forestry where there is rough or steep country to traverse.

A log suspended from cables on the spar is swung into position to load onto the bogies. Behind the spar is a stack of logs waiting to be loaded. Originally both log hauler and lokey would have been steam, but for a variety of reasons – fire rules, old locomotives wearing out, efficiency – diesels had largely taken over the last of the bush trams and their loading sites in the 1950s.

The Journey to the Mill, Ruatapu, 1959

Even as late as November 1959 Butler Bros had been extending their trams across the pakihi and cutover bush to reach another loading site. Although the earthworks are kept to a minimum (note the grade), the track is well laid and ballasted, a desirable feature with the heavier and rigid wheel-based diesel lokeys. This line lasted less than a year, until the whole tram system closed in 1960. With roads built by the Forest Service giving good access to skid sites, it was not economic to keep the tram running.

The Dispatch Foundry, in Greymouth, was experienced in designing and manufacturing bush lokeys. Here, one is climbing very slowly (and noisily) toward the mill at Ruatapu. While it had an enclosed cab, two old mattresses were in the back in an attempt to reduce the noise of a high-revving diesel as it pulled its train of logs up the grade. This lokey, or one similar, spent the last years of its life shunting in the yard at Ruatapu, until the Hokitika-Ross line closed in 1980.

Bridges, viaducts, tunnels and even spirals were all features of bush trams in their heyday, as sawmillers tried to reach rich stands of timber with the least possible earthworks.

This long bridge on the Ruatapu train could not be avoided. As with the rest of Butler's tram routes – at least on the 'main line' – it was solidly built, and included in the section at the bottom of the photograph is a former New Zealand Railways turntable used as a girder over the river.

Mamaku Bush Tram, 1963

Mamaku, on a plateau 22 kilometres northwest of Rotorua, and reached by rail via a 12-kilometre grade as steep as 1: 35 in places on the Rotorua side, has a long and rich history of sawmilling. The Mamaku Forest was – and still is in places – extensive and was penetrated for many years by bush trams bringing timber into the mills near Mamaku railway station.

New Zealand Railways Stores Branch had a mill, and many staff, based at Mamaku from the 1940s to the sale of the mill in 1974. The 'tram', which ran out to the forest, was built to a high standard, comparable to a light traffic branch line. For many years a local contractor, Ollie Smith, a man of great mechanical ingenuity, rebuilt truck chassis onto railway wheels, and these provided the motive power for both the New Zealand Railways logging operation and some of the other mills, including Gamman's, which lasted until the mid-1960s.

Gamman's tram was much more in the light railway tradition. In August 1963, when these photographs were taken, the jigger was limited to about 12 kph (on the 'big' New Zealand Railways tram, 30 kph was no problem). It was to be the final phase of the tram's operation.

This photograph shows the jigger nearing the mill on the Gamman's tram, in a cutting of cutover bush; the other is of the Railways' tram, where one remaining tall tree stands as a sentinel amongst the regrowth.

A modern plant, milling exotic timber, still operates at Mamaku, and an example of Ollie Smith's ingenuity with bush lokeys has been restored and is displayed at the north end of the village.

Orongorongo Water Supply, Wainuiomata, 1997

Small railways have a significant history in both the construction and maintenance of water supply projects up until the 1940s. Dam construction and pipeline maintenance in the Waitakere Ranges in West Auckland depended on such lines, some of which remain today as tourist ventures.

Wellington has still, although in truncated form, a 610mm gauge line operating in the Orongorongo Ranges, behind Wainuiomata. The railway was originally built in the 1920s to enable construction materials and staff to go through rather than over a substantial hill (the tunnel is four kilometres long) and beyond that to reach the various water intake sites and to provide access for a site caretaker.

Today, only the tunnel section of the line is still in service, as a road has been built over the hill to provide access for construction and maintenance work in the river valley. And the advent of helicopters has eased the task of transporting materials to inaccessible sites.

The narrow valleys where the tunnel emerges meant that a turntable rather than a curve had to be used to service the tracks along the valley. The photograph shows the original route not long before it was pulled out in 1997 to allow a new pipeline to be built. In the distance is a single-span wooden truss bridge, rebuilt as part of the same project. The train crossed the bridge, traversed a further section of the valley and passed through a short tunnel. It terminated at the far end of the tunnel. It was there to facilitate the use of railed vehicles in a confined space while maintaining water pipelines inside tunnels.

In the same 1990s project the existing tramway in the four-kilometre tunnel was rebuilt, the pipeline was replaced, and a new jigger has since been built in Wellington Regional Council workshops. The tram is still used regularly for access to the intakes and for maintenance checks on the major pipeline through the tunnel.

The Gasworks Railway, Wellington, 1964

Almost every New Zealand town of any size had a coal-fired gas works, many established in the 19th century. Towns as small as Waipawa, Waimate and Masterton each boasted their own gas works. In 1916 there were 56 coal gas plants in New Zealand.

Smaller plants began to close from the 1940s onward, usually as the equipment and/or pipelines wore out. The advent of natural gas effectively closed all North Island plants in the 1960s, and ageing plant and infrastructure, as well as more efficient alternative fuels, saw the remaining South Island plants closed until the last coal-fired plant, Dunedin, ceased producing coal gas in 1987. It was the last such plant in New Zealand and now one of only two coal gas plant museums in the world.

Many of the larger 'gas works', as they were known, had their own siding or small railway linking their sites to the railway system. Dunedin, Christchurch, Wellington and Auckland all had small locomotives for shunting the coal, and coke where relevant, between New Zealand Railways or a wharf and the plant, and within the worksite itself.

The Wellington railway ran from Miramar Wharf (still extant) along Miramar Avenue through the cutting, and swung south into the extensive gas works site. As much of the railway was on the street, it was laid with tramway rail, to keep the flange path clear and provide a smoother surface for motor vehicles. It was built to 1220mm gauge, the rather unusual gauge used by Wellington electric tramways.

Colliers from Newcastle, Australia, would berth at Miramar Wharf, the coal would be unloaded by grab into hoppers, and a small steam locomotive would take a short train back into the gas works for discharge – a distance of about a kilometre. The complex track work was there to allow multiple train movements on and off the wharf and along the route. From the outbreak of war in 1939 coal came from West Coast mines and was trucked from the coal wharf near Wellington railway station. The Miramar Wharf tramway was not used after that date, but the two locomotives and 10 hopper wagons continued to work inside the site until the early 1950s. The locomotives and wagons were scrapped in 1954. The track remained in the road until 1966, about the time that the gas works were closed and the site redeveloped.

Tokomaru Bay, North Island East Coast, 1967

The East Coast of the North Island, beyond Gisborne, was for many years one of the more isolated parts of New Zealand. Road construction was difficult, with a demanding topography and geology to deal with. Road maintenance was expensive; there was a lack of good quality road metal in the area, and the region's farm economy was largely extensive pastoral holdings with a low ratepayer base for funding better access.

One of the results was the continuing use of small, mainly coastal shipping ports until the post-World War II years when both roads and the capacity of trucks began to improve. Tolaga Bay, Tokomaru Bay and Hicks Bay were the three major examples, each with a wharf, storage sheds and a light railway to link stores, wharf and, in the case of Tokomaru Bay, a sizeable freezing works.

The photographs show, first, the Tokomaru Bay freezing works, which closed in 1952, and the remains of the 915mm gauge railway inside what was left of the works in 1967. The remainder of the line served a large and distinguished cargo shed once owned by the New Zealand Shipping Co. The route length was about 1.5 kilometres, but the many additional tracks would have brought the total to over two kilometres.

The railway opened in 1911, the same year as a slaughter house. It was variously

operated over its history by small steam and diesel locomotives and once had some 25 wagons used for carrying coal, wool, skins and general cargo. The Harbour Master, Captain Peter McCallum, and one of his small team are shown admiring their train on the lawn outside Captain McCallum's house. This was possibly their last train (May 1967) as the last commercial use of the railway was in 1966.

Why use a railway, and not trucks or wagons? A railway track on a long narrow wharf is the safest and most reliable way of handling cargo. Even today on fishing wharves in some smaller ports, including in Australia, small trolleys on rails are manhandled for this reason. Secondly, when the port was opened, rail was the dominant mode, and it was sensible to adapt it (on a smaller scale) to meet the demands of cargo handling, especially where the port's immediate hinterland provided the production, sorting and storage areas. And industrial railways on that scale were then the norm: small locomotives, both steam and diesel, were readily available.

From the early 1960s better roads and bigger trucks saw freight being carried to Gisborne for direct loading onto overseas ships or railed to processing plants further south. The last coastal shipping services on the East Coast ran to about 1964. The small ports and their quite substantial wharves, now in somewhat decrepit condition, remain today as monuments to a former era in transport methods – and the usefulness of the small railway.

Cumberland Street, Dunedin, 1969

This is perhaps the ultimate 'local' or little railway: the spur leading from a network siding into a grain and seed store via a wagon turntable, and the transfer from a standard wagon to a trolley for the last leg of the journey across busy Cumberland Street into the seed store. Perhaps the turntable was not working, or only a few sacks needed to be transferred. Usually the wagon would have been taken into the store, towed by a tractor or horse.

There were many such wagon turntables along Cumberland Street (and elsewhere in the South Island) where in 1969 tracks for freight storage and transfer came right to the Cumberland Street boundary. The turntables allowed access to not only grain and seed stores, but large wool stores, at least one of which had another turntable inside the building to allow railway wagon access to other parts of the store. *George Emerson*

Chapter Seven

CASE STUDIES

The case studies that follow summarise the events leading to the closure of three rural branch lines:

- The 35-kilometre Oxford branch in Canterbury served a mixed farming area close to Christchurch.

- The Moutohora branch near Gisborne, 79 kilometres long, closed in 1959 after a significant role in developing areas of both intensive farming and hill country, as well as carrying native timber and road metal.

- The Waimate branch in South Canterbury, only 7 kilometres long, served a prosperous and intensively farmed area and Waimate itself, the district's local commercial and distribution centre.

The Oxford Branch, Canterbury

The Oxford branch railway was completed in 1875. The junction with the main line was at Rangiora, 33 kilometres from Christchurch. The more direct road route, from near Kaiapoi to Bennetts and thence to Oxford, is significantly shorter and placed the Oxford district within some 55 kilometres of Christchurch. Today, a truck can traverse this route within an hour. The distance by rail from Christchurch to Oxford was 68 kilometres.

The main reason for building this line was to give access to extensive stands of timber in the Oxford district. By the 1880s most of the timber had been cut for milling or burned to clear the land for pasture. The major traffic on the line became grain, livestock and other farm produce, with fertiliser and general goods making up most of the traffic into the district.

Rural industry and trading were well represented along the line, if on a small scale. Near Stoke there was a flour mill; Cust and Oxford saw regular stock sales; Carleton was the loading point for a nearby flax mill. Four of the stations – Bennetts, Cust, East Oxford and West Oxford – handled sufficient traffic to warrant staff until 1931. (There was a stationmaster at East Oxford until the early 1950s.) Locomotive and train crews were originally based at West Oxford and Bennetts, in the latter case to work the Eyreton branch to Kaiapoi.

Cust, on the Oxford Branch, in the last months of the line's life in 1959.
Photographer unknown

In 1894 the line was extended from West Oxford to meet the Malvern branch (now the Midland line) at Sheffield. This was seen as the start of a planned inland Canterbury main line, running along the foothills of the plains to north of Timaru, but there was no construction beyond this 18.5-kilometre section. It carried little traffic and was closed in July 1930. The road bridge across the Waimakariri River near Sheffield is the only significant remnant; it was built for both the road and railway.

Scheduled passenger traffic on the Rangiora-Oxford section ceased in February 1931, and staff were withdrawn from all stations except East Oxford. The locomotive depots on the branch closed, and trains were worked from Christchurch or Rangiora. The frequency of freight services was reduced over the years, until after 1945 only two trains a week ran on the branch, with occasional specials for livestock or grain traffic. This was further reduced to a weekly service in the 1950s, supplemented by specials as required. By this time the line was carrying only a fraction of the district's produce, essentially grain and fertiliser. But farmer loyalty held on (supported by the transport licensing regulations), and as late as February 1959 a consignment of some 450 ewes was received at East Oxford from the Amberley ewe fair – a journey of some 52 kilometres.

Competition and Closure

Commercial road freight and passenger services had operated in the district since the early 1920s, taking most of the line's passenger traffic and an increasingly significant proportion of the freight. Fuel and tyre shortages during World War II saw the decline level out, but in 1946 road competition became even stronger when Oxford Transport Service Ltd began operations. By 1958 the company was operating a general goods service throughout the district with 12 vehicle authorities. Some years earlier the company had received an exemption from the 30-mile protection clause, allowing the road cartage of livestock to freezing works in the Christchurch area and to Addington saleyards. But it was not until the branch line was closed that one of the key commodities – fertiliser – could legally be carried from the plant at Hornby, south of Christchurch, to Oxford.

The branch's hinterland's wool clip was carried to Christchurch wool stores by Oxford Transport, by farmers' lorries or by Langford Motors' daily freight run to and from Christchurch. This firm, which in 1958 operated two vehicles, was permitted to carry general goods between Oxford and Christchurch.

A glance at the map on page 10 showing the impact of the 30 and 40-mile boundary from Christchurch, shows clearly the increasing irrelevance of the Oxford branch to the district's transport needs as improved road transport supplied a more frequent and efficient service. But there was still a residual loyalty from some landholders, and it was not easy for a government department to summarily close a railway that had been for many years a part of the district's transport network.

For Railways' management of the time the message was clear: keep the line operating at a minimal level, and close it when expenditure was needed. This was reflected in the Minister of Railways' statement announcing the decision to close the line:

"... Most of the sleepers are almost useless, sleeper renewals costing £55,000 [$110,000] are essential. Little use is being made of the line, and the need for it appears to have passed. The whole area is extensively served by road operators over good-quality shingle and sealed roads. At two centres, Oxford and Cust, there are 155 heavy trucks, 97 light trucks and 106 trailers registered, and 95 per cent of these are owned by farmers. Last year [1958] one tenth of the wool grown in the area was carried by rail. It is estimated that there could be an 80 per cent increase in wool [carried] this year, but this would produce only £107 [$214] in revenue." (*The Press*, Christchurch, 28 January 1959)

The 1952 Royal Commission on Railways saw the Oxford branch as a line where the possibilities of using a cheap diesel-mechanical locomotive could be tested. The Commission suggested that when this was done the service frequency be managed to cater for the expected growth in traffic following the closure of the Eyreton branch (in May 1954). Nothing was done toward implementing this proposal.

Given the regional and district geography of settlement, particularly the proximity to Christchurch, it was unlikely that even a daily service would match the convenience of road transport, let alone the comparative prices. The locomotive would have been better used in a busy marshalling yard.

The major factor in the closure of the Oxford branch was the district's closeness to the major regional centre, Christchurch. Almost all the traffic to and from branch line stations was to or from stations in the Christchurch urban area. Given that railways are essentially a longer haul and/or heavy traffic mode, the line had simply become irrelevant. It had served its function as a developmental line, especially over a period of some 40 years when rail was the most reliable and practical form of transport

For perhaps another 30 years, until the 1950s, it had some diminishing utility. But as commercial functions centralised on Rangiora and Christchurch with the withdrawal of those functions from Oxford and other rural centres, as roads improved, as almost every family had a car and most farms a truck, a lightly used railway was no longer needed. It had outlived its usefulness to its community.

The line was formally closed from 18 April 1959. But in that month there was a final burst of activity, with several trainloads of pine logs being loaded at West Oxford and Bennetts. This was one of the first consignments of export pine logs from Canterbury.

The closure was marked by protests more political than passionate. The district ignored the last train and soon forgot about the local railway except as a curiosity of an earlier age. However, 45 years later it was intriguing to see the local heritage trail using station name boards at former station sites and marking in particular Bennetts and Cust station sites. A few goods sheds remain on private land, but otherwise the formation and fittings have been demolished or merged quietly with the local landscape.

THE MOUTOHORA BRANCH

The 79-kilometre line between Gisborne and Moutohora (Motuhora until 1951) was completed in 1917 and closed in 1959. In contrast to the Oxford branch, it served an area of developing hill country farms. At the time of closure the main road serving the last 32 kilometres of the branch was in poor condition, and the district served by the line contained much land only marginally economic for farming, a state of affairs caused partly by the high costs of transporting fertiliser and other farm stores, as well as by the physical characteristics of the rugged hill country being farmed.

The major point of interest about the Moutohora branch, then, is the reason for its closure at a time when much local farm land was still being developed – an activity in which for many years the assistance of the railway has been regarded as essential. A second point is the fact that part of the line lay well beyond 30 miles (48 kilometres) from the district market and regional centre, Gisborne, and the railway was thus legally assured of most traffic from this portion of the branch.

In spite of these factors, the case for closure was on several grounds a reasonable one.

Otoko, north of Gisborne, on the Moutohora branch, a few months before closure in 1959. The state highway was built across this site shortly afterwards.

Traffic trends

From the time the first part of the line was opened in 1902 until the Napier-Gisborne line was completed to Gisborne in 1942, the Moutohora line (until 1942 the Gisborne section) fulfilled an entirely local function in serving the district's residents and carrying the district's produce to Gisborne. Passenger and freight traffic was heavy in the early years of operation and the line consistently showed a healthy operating profit. In the 1920 financial year, the peak year for livestock traffic, 174,000 head of sheep and 2180 cattle moved over the line. Other farm produce, inward consignments of stores and fertiliser, a steady flow of road metal from the quarries at Moutohora (then the only source of reasonable quality metal in the Gisborne district) and large amounts of timber moved down the steeply graded line to Gisborne, a pattern of traffic flow maintained until the end of World War II. Motor competition had made some inroads, especially in the late 1920s, but the protection provided by the legislation of 1936 held a lot of traffic to the railway. And the quality of the local roads did not encourage cheap road haulage.

In 1945 regular passenger services were withdrawn. Competition for freight intensified, and increasing quantities of traffic, especially livestock, were carried to Gisborne by road. The 1952 Royal Commission on Railways dealt with the branch at some length, pointing out that the line was then still carrying some 20,000 tons of road metal a year, as well as livestock, logs, wool, fertiliser (from New Plymouth and Wanganui) and other traffic. The commission noted that the main highway, which ran close to the line as far as Matawai (71 kilometres), would be "structurally unable to carry the traffic diverted to it by closing the line", and they considered that:

> "In the national interest it will be necessary to continue the services by this line for a further period of two years . . ."

The commission also noted that:

> "The answer to whether the line be eventually retained appears to depend on the settlers themselves and other interested parties who would be affected."

Expenditure on maintenance and renewals declined, and the result was a steady deterioration in the condition of the track and facilities at stations. The running down process had begun.

Closure – and protests

In February 1959 the Minister of Railways announced that the Moutohora line was to be closed a few weeks later, on 14 March. He pointed out that the line needed £325,000 ($650,000) spent on it in the next few years and that traffic on the line had dwindled to such a level that the railway was no longer worth retaining.

District reactions were varied. Many Gisborne organisations and district local authorities expressed regret but accepted the points set out by the Minister. Settlers at the end of the line, however, did not share this attitude, and well-attended meetings at Matawai raised strong protests at the proposed closure. Later, Gisborne interests, particularly those connected with farmers, emerged from their apathy to add support to the farmers' arguments.

The case for retention of the railway included a number of major points:

- There was no serious alternative service available as the main road was unsealed, narrow, hilly and in poor condition, and it included a number of bridges with low axle load limits.

- The rapidly increasing use of superphosphate on local farms, a trend encouraged by the cheaper superphosphate obtainable from the new fertiliser works at Napier and the growth of aerial topdressing activities in the district, would be inhibited by the extra transport charges imposed if the line closed. The loss of the railway would, it was claimed, increase fertiliser application costs by 9/- [nine shillings = 90 cents] an acre.

A number of other very general points were raised, few of which had any direct relevance to the issue.

To a certain extent the points raised by the Matawai settlers have been resolved since the line closed. Heavy expenditure on the main road brought it up to a standard that enabled more economic road haulage. (This expenditure would have been necessary even if the line had stayed, as the road is part of the increasingly busy Gisborne-Opotiki main highway.) It is impossible to assess precisely the effect of the railway closing on local farm production – although the Land Utilisation Survey of the Gisborne-East Coast area published in 1964 did not mention the closing of the line as having affected in any way the development of farming in the area. The survey regarded overseas prices for farm produce as a much more potent influence on the level of expenditure on fertiliser.

The assertion about lack of service inevitably appears at protest meetings about branch line closures. While it is perhaps fair to say that the Railways had not gone out of their way to attract custom, they had made an attempt to offer a service that met the normal demand to be expected from customers along the line. At times of seasonal peaks Moutohora branch settlers, along with farmers in other parts of the country, at times had wagon orders delayed – but this is a fact of life in a railway system subjected to the sudden fluctuations of demand experienced in a farm-based economy. Road transport faces the same problem at periods of peak demand.

Railways economics or regional development?

Operating economics dictated that a decision had to be made, about 1959, as to whether the branch was to be retained for five or ten years, or whether it was to be closed immediately. The decision had effectively been taken in 1952, after the publication of the Royal Commission's report. In the eyes of the Commission, and of New Zealand Railways, railway resources were being wasted in keeping the Moutohora line in operation any longer.

The case of the Moutohora line poses questions that did not arise with the Oxford branch, or with similar short lines serving well-established farming areas. The decision to close the line was taken before the Land Utilisation Survey was started and at a time when farm production was increasing at a rapid rate. Regarded solely from the point of view of railway operating economics, however, the decision to close the Moutohora line was reasonable. But it marked a significant change from the attitudes held in earlier decades, when a line such as this would have been seen as having a clearly developmental role. The closure represented a threshold in the role of railways and their role in rural areas.

Moutohora Branch Goods Traffic

Year ending 31 March, 1959

(with estimated number of lorry loads to carry equivalent traffic assuming road and bridge restrictions in force at the time of closure)

Commodity		**Lorry Loads**
Cattle	9500 head	633
Sheep	32,000 head	266
Timber	46,000 super feet (102 tons)	11
Superphosphate	14,000 tons	1166
Road metal	29,000 tons	2071
Cream	600 tons	120
Other goods	12,000 tons	2400

Source: *Gisborne Herald* 30 April 1959

The Waimate branch line terminal at a seasonal peak in March 1961. It is Sunday, and a picnic train waits at the platform for its passengers to return in the afternoon. Nearly every suitable wagon has been loaded with wheat on Saturday: there is a line of sheep wagons on the back road ready for the Waihao Downs Ewe Fair, with its regular consignments to mid-Canterbury stations at Lyndhurst and Chertsey. And the carpenter is based there for a few weeks, with his tool shed, accommodation and materials wagon by the goods shed.

The Waimate Branch

This third case study deals with a very short line – the seven-kilometre branch from Studholme (39 kilometres south of Timaru) to the market town and service centre of Waimate.

The line was opened in 1877. From the early 1880s until its closure in 1953 a 13-kilometre extension served the small settlements of Waihao Forks and Waihao Downs and the prosperous down country through the Waimate Gorge. In 1961 closure of the Studholme-Waimate line was proposed, but after strong local objections the subject was allowed to drop until late in 1965. In spite of further protests from the district, the branch was closed on 31 March 1966.

This was the first time that a branch line closure had affected a town the size of Waimate (3310 in the 1961 census), and the implications of such an abandonment are of some interest.

Traffic trends

Scheduled passenger services on both the Waimate and Waimate Downs branches ceased from 9 February 1931; only picnic and other special trains had brought passengers to or from Waimate by rail since then. Road transport had made inroads into branch goods traffic from the early 1920s, but the petrol and tyre shortages of World War II saw increased use of the two lines. Livestock traffic diminished after 1945, and other goods traffic dropped sharply from 1952-53 after the Waihao Downs line was closed. The total traffic remained at about 20,000 tons a year until the Studholme-Waimate branch line closed in 1966.

Much of the goods traffic to and from Waimate was concerned with the function of Waimate borough as the commercial and trading centre for most of Waimate County, a large and prosperous farming district containing 6058 residents at the 1961 census. The county was served by stock and station agencies, general merchants, road transport operators, retail outlets and professional and educational services in Waimate; the administrative centre of the county was also in the town. Thus, Waimate was the focal point for a much wider area than just the borough, and as a railhead and headquarters of the district's road transport operators, a considerable quantity of goods for farms, as well as for borough residents, was channelled through the railway station.

The composition of the branch line traffic reflected this function. But of even more interest were the origins and destinations of goods traffic moving to and from Waimate. The general pattern was one in which the great majority of consignments to Waimate came from places over 160 kilometres away, while much of the outward traffic moved relatively short distances (to Timaru and Oamaru). However, about two-thirds of the outward consignments, mainly grain, moved at the busiest time of the year for all transport modes. (See Waimate Branch Goods Traffic table on page 100 for a summary of traffic flows)

The cases for and against closure

The Railways' case rested on the usual points:

- The line was showing an operating loss – some £8000 ($16,000) in the year ending 31 March 1961.

- The track would shortly need new sleepers and other maintenance expenditure.

- Traffic in the longer term had declined (although over a short term it appeared that the annual tonnages had levelled off at about 20,000 tons a year).

- The main line was only seven kilometres away by road, and in the circumstances the retention of the short line to Waimate seemed unnecessary.

The major points of the case against closure were:

- The length of the line hardly justified the title 'branch line'. It was rather an extended siding, and it was irrelevant to apply branch line accounting methods to such a situation. The same approach should have been adopted toward the line's operation and costing as toward the servicing of an industry at the end of a lengthy private siding.

- The Waimate line served a market town and service centre of considerable importance to the surrounding district. It was not, as was the case with many other lines closed, a 'spur' line serving a scattered farming community.

Other submissions were related to different – and cheaper – methods of working the line, a matter in which Railways admitted there was room for improvement, but they could not see their way clear to change existing methods at the time. There were many other subjects for discussion, but the bases of the arguments revolved around the two major points mentioned above and, increasingly, around the function of Waimate in the urban hierarchy and the effect – if any – on this function if the link to the national railway system was cut.

The discussion was, in effect, carried on at two levels. The Railways argued strongly on the basis of operating economics, with passing reference to the function of the railway in the district. The local residents argued from the basis of the railway's importance to the district, with passing – and at times irrelevant – reference to operating economics.

Unfortunately, neither side ever gave much public indication of recognising the merit of each other's arguments and of trying to reach a compromise. The result was the closure of the line on 31 March 1966.

Waimate Branch Goods Traffic

Year ending 31 March, 1961

	Inward		**Outward**	
	Tons	Per Cent	Tons	Per Cent
Livestock	10	..	332	6
Timber	1240	8	-	-
Coal	5771	37	10	..
Fertiliser	2984	19	11	..
Grain and seed	178	1	3472	65
Root crops	50	..	532	10
Wool	-	..	219	4
Bitumen	437	3	-	-
Small lots	1657	11	351	7
Other goods	3080	20	439	8
	15,407	100	5366	100

Notes: *Livestock and timber tonnages are estimates based on the number of livestock and the footage of timber.*
Dots indicate less than half of one per cent.
After 1961 livestock traffic declined with the lifting of competitive restrictions, the tonnage of coal fell by about one third with the closing of the local gas works, and fertiliser, grain and timber traffic all increased. The result was a total figure of, still, about 20,000 tons a year.
Source: New Zealand Railways

Waimate Branch Origins and Destination of Traffic

Inward Traffic

Timber	Mainly indigenous timber from West Coast (there was a short term traffic in logs from North Canterbury in 1965-66)
Coal	From Buller, Reefton and Grey fields on the West Coast, and from the Ohai and Kaitangata fields of Southland and South Otago respectively
Fertiliser	From Ravensbourne, near Dunedin
Bitumen	From Lyttelton, to a bulk depot in the railway yards
Other goods	Cement – from Burnside (Dunedin), Westport, and Orawia (Southland) Steel – from Dunedin or Timaru Seed – from Timaru or other Canterbury depots Posts – from Addington or Culverden (North Canterbury)
Small lots	Mainly from Christchurch and especially Dunedin

Outward Traffic

Grain	Wheat – mainly to mills at or near Oamaru, Timaru and, in later years, a few bulk consignments via the rail ferry to the North Island Barley – to Ashburton and Heathcote
Root crops	Mainly potatoes to Timaru and Oamaru for shipment to the North Island. Again, this traffic was increasingly attracted to the rail ferry
Wool	Largely to Dunedin, a little to Timaru
Small lots	Mainly vegetables and such items as kegs, gas cylinders etc to Dunedin, to a lesser extent to Timaru

The point is clear. A large proportion of Waimate branch traffic was not 'local'; it moved from major centres to Waimate in its role as a district market town and distribution point. In this respect it could well be argued that the Waimate branch could have played a small but significant continuing role in the national transport service provided by the railways at that time. But over the longer term, with the increasing centralisation of commercial activities in major centres, the line would have become irrelevant.

EPILOGUE

A century ago railways and other forms of public transport provided most people with their means of travel over journeys of any distance. In 2004 it is a little difficult to imagine a life with few motor vehicles and dependency for recreational travel on scheduled train, ferry and tram services – or walking and cycling.

The *Otago Daily Times* in 2004 published a short report from 1904, a reprint in their "100 Years Ago" column. It gave a pen picture of how Dunedin people used their railways (and no doubt their trams and cable cars to reach the railway) for a day's outing at Easter 1904. Dunedin's population at the time was about 59,000.

> "The prospect of fine weather for the Easter holidays was unfortunately not fulfilled, and the rain which fell pretty steadily yesterday morning doubtless caused many to stay at home who would have preferred a trip to the country. The principal attraction for residents of the city was the race meeting at Mosgiel, to which about 625 persons journeyed by rail; and next in public favour was the show at Middlemarch, to which place some 200 people traveled. The total number of tickets issued at the local railway station during the day was about 3200, which must be considered very satisfactory, taking everything into account. About 60 passengers were booked to Christchurch, and some 90 to Oamaru, while about 50 went to Palmerston, and nearly 70 to Waikouaiti. Seacliff appears to be a very popular holiday resort, and no less than 260 passengers journeyed there, while about 120 travelled to Waitati, and about 40 to Puketeraki, and a similar number to Warrington. A little more than 200 tickets were issued to Mosgiel Junction, the purchasers of some no doubt going to the races, and on the branch lines – Lawrence, Catlins River, and Otago Central – about 400 people were carried. Port Chalmers was also well patronized, some 240 tickets being issued. A large number of excursionists journeyed to Henley by the morning train, and thence by the launch Waiwera to Taieri Mouth. The railway officials have had an arduous and trying time in attending to the wants of the public during the holidays, and they are entitled to a meed of praise for the manner in which they have fulfilled their duties."

In the five decades that this book covers, population numbers and the patterns of people's travel have changed significantly from the times of the *Otago Daily Times* report. There are now many more private cars, and buses had begun to complement and eventually replace trams and cable cars. And roads were improving rapidly.

Within this half-century there were the last (almost) of the picnic and excursion trains run by the national rail operator, though independent train operators have to some extent filled the gap. Regular express trains between metropolitan and regional centres now traverse only three routes compared to the ten covered in the 1950s. The last of the local rural passenger and mixed trains have vanished. The movement of and demand for freight services experienced radical change. Suburban and local passenger trains remain only in Auckland and Wellington regions compared to the seven areas serviced in the 1940s.

One can debate endlessly the improvements in quality of life and economic benefit wrought by this process of change. Equally, one can look back to it as a period of less pressure, as rather more structured and orderly, and as a time of living within smaller and more cohesive communities.

Nostalgia is justified in such a context. But nostalgia is nearly always an exercise in selective memory. It is usually pleasant, and at times instructive, to look back, to reflect, from the comforts of a more modern age. This book has aimed to encourage such reflection.

Sources

The commentaries are based on my own knowledge of both New Zealand's railways and an understanding bred from reading about, listening to and observation of the rural economy. Where dates and specifics were needed, there are a few essential references. These include:

Dangerfield, J.A. and Emerson, G.W., *Over the Garden Wall,* the story of the Otago Central Railway, Otago Railway and Locomotive Society, 1995

Dew, Leslie, *The Great Northern: The Story of the Waiau Branch Railway*, Weka Pass Railway, 2001

Distance Tables, North and South Island, Showing Distance Between all Railway Stations within each Island, New Zealand Railways, 1974

Geographical Mileage Table, 1957, New Zealand Railways

Gradient Diagrams, North Island and South Island, New Zealand Railways, various dates

Johnston, Albert B., Startup, Robert, Berry, Allan P. (editor), *Mail by Rail in New Zealand*, Royal Philatelic Society of New Zealand, 2001

McQueen, Euan, *Report on the Rural Branch Line*, MA Thesis, Victoria University of Wellington, 1966

Mahoney, Paul, *The Era of the Bush Tram in New Zealand,* IPL Books, 1998

New Zealand Railway and Tramway Atlas, 4th Edition, The Quail Map Company, 1993

New Zealand Railway Observer, Journal of the NZ Railways & Locomotive Society, 1944 - present.

New Zealand Railways Working Timetables, North Island Main Line and Branches, South Island Main Line and Branches, various editions

New Zealand Railways Working Timetable, North Island 1947, facsimile reproduction, New Zealand Railway and Locomotive Society, 1985

New Zealand Railways Working Timetable, South Island 1952, 1974 facsimile reproduction, New Zealand Railway and Locomotive Society, 1979

Railways, Corporate Services, Accession W3495 Archives New Zealand / Te Rua Mahara o te Kawanotanga Wellington Office (photographs of Motuhora and Methven).

Reid, R C (Bob), *One More Mile on the NZR,* the Junction Press, 2003

Research Note

Number of Stations

The tally of stations open for general freight traffic is derived from information in the New Zealand Railways Working Timetables at the time. The coding of station functions is generally explicit, though at the margin there can be doubt in a few cases as to whether a station is able to handle general freight, or freight only for one major customer. Hence the rounding of the totals in the text.

The figures for stations at the start of the period under review are from facsimile reproductions of the Working Timetables for North Island (July 1947) and South Island (December 1952). There are likely to have been some minor additions or deletions to the number of stations within that five year period – the opening of the Kinleith branch in 1950, with additional stations, is a case in point – but the figures presented give an order of magnitude that allows a reasonable comparison with the current situation.

There were in the 1950s over 150 small stations handling passengers and/or small lots of freight and parcels, but not wagon-loads as there was no siding. The information about these is from the same sources. Again, it is difficult to be precise about an exact number because of the coding used in the Working Timetables.

INDEX

D

E

F

G

H

I

J

K

L

M

N

O

P

Q

R

S